Fire
in my bones

FIRE
in my bones
A Study in Faith and Belief

by C. Robert Mesle

I used to say, "I will not think about him, I will not speak in his name any more." Then there seemed to be a fire burning in my heart, imprisoned in my bones. The effort to restrain it wearied me, I could not bear it.—Jeremiah 20:9 Jerusalem Bible

---

Christian Education Commission
Reorganized Church of Jesus Christ of Latter Day Saints

herald house

• p.o. box hh • 3225 south noland road • independence, missouri 64055 •

Copyright © 1984
Herald Publishing House
Independence, Missouri

All rights in this book are reserved. No part of the text may be reproduced in any form without written permission of the publisher, except brief quotations used in connection with reviews in magazines or newspapers.

Library of Congress Cataloging in Publication Data

Mesle, C. Robert.
   Fire in my bones.

   "Christian Education Commission, Reorganized Church of Jesus Christ of Latter Day Saints."
   1. Faith. I. Reorganized Church of Jesus Christ of Latter Day Saints. Christian Education Commission. II. Title.
BT771.2.M45   1984   234'.2   83-22821
ISBN 0-8309-0387-9

Printed in the United States of America

TABLE OF CONTENTS

Foreword 7
Preface 9
Acknowledgments 13
Editor's Introduction 15
An Opening Activity 19

Part I: DEFINITION AND EXAMPLE
   Chapter   1. Introduction: Faith as
                  Commitment 22
   Chapter   2. Faith as Being Grasped: My
                  Experience with Sarah 34

Part II: WORKING OUT SOME DETAILS
   Chapter   3. The Kaleidoscope of Faith 48
   Chapter   4. Faith and Hope 63
   Chapter   5. Faith and Trust 70
   Chapter   6. Faith and Love 78
   Chapter   7. Faith and Belief 85

Part III: APPLICATIONS TO CHRISTIAN FAITH
   Introduction to Part III: Faith and Belief 96
   Chapter   8. Faith, Belief, and God, Part 1 99
   Chapter   9. Faith, Belief, and God, Part 2 110
   Chapter 10. Faith in the Church 121
   Chapter 11. Faith in the Scriptures 132
   Chapter 12. Faith in Christ 148

Part IV: FAITH AND BELIEF: A HISTORY OF
   THE WORDS
   Chapter 13. Faith and Belief in the English
                  Language and the Bible 162
   Chapter 14. The Biblical Language of
                  Faith and Belief 170
   Chapter 15. Implications: Biblical Faith
                  and Modern Belief 182

Part V: FURTHER THOUGHTS
　　Chapter 16. "The Creative Role of Doubt in Religion" (a reprint of an article by Robert Baird, with a comment and further thoughts by by Robert Mesle). 198
　　Chapter 17. Two Types of Theology 222
　　Chapter 18. Faith, Freedom, and Growth 241
A Closing Activity 252

FOREWORD

The author of *Fire in My Bones* considers in depth a fundamental concept of Christianity: *faith*. Each reader who becomes immersed in this study can expect to be affected by its message. Some will be challenged and stretched; some will be affirmed; still others may be led to examine their faith and the basis on which it is grounded. We trust that exposure to this material will fulfill the author's hope that persons will discover a dynamic faith which will set them free and cause them to grow.

We recognize that much of the material may be difficult for some readers. In this book, however, Robert Mesle provides students with sound ideas which are amply illustrated and a solid foundation from which exploration of this and similar issues may continue.

Fire in My Bones is a thorough, systematic, and enriching study of faith and belief—two building blocks of a rewarding and fulfilling life experience. We encourage its study by those who are willing to confront, examine, and struggle with the issues it raises. A mature faith must undergo this kind of rigorous examination.

                        THE FIRST PRESIDENCY

                              Wallace B. Smith
                              Howard S. Sheehy, Jr.
                              Alan D. Tyree

PREFACE

The title of this book is taken from the words of the prophet Jeremiah. They suggest both the struggle and the power of faith. Jeremiah uttered them while wrestling at the most basic level with the depth of his own faith. Just when he cried out against God for having deceived and seduced him, just when he had resolved to abandon all commitment to the proclamation of justice, he discovered that he could not escape the call which had grasped his life.

> I used to say, "I will not think about him, I will not speak in his name any more." Then there seemed to be a fire burning in my heart, imprisoned in my bones. The effort to restrain it wearied me, I could not bear it.—Jeremiah 20:9 JB

My struggle to understand the nature of faith began when I feared that I might be losing mine. Long thought and careful study led me to conclude that I was not losing my faith at all, but only some particular beliefs. I was misled by a common assumption that I could be faithful only by holding certain beliefs. That assumption caused a great deal of pain, for it implied that there might be some conflict between faith and intellectual integrity. I encounter the same misunderstanding and concern in most people with whom I discuss faith.

No conflict exists, however, between the integrity of honest inquiry and the commitment of faith. They are not rivals, but partners in the life of the human spirit when that life is whole and creative. Doubt is not the opposite of faith, but its tool when faith has the courage to seek the truth about itself and that which it seeks to serve. Faith does not deny or suppress doubt or inquiry, but uses them to bring about growth of understanding, depth of insight, and more effective commitment.

The understanding of faith which generates so

much trouble is of faith as belief without evidence, or even against the evidence. When they think about it for five or ten minutes, most people sense that there is something wrong and destructive about this definition. In my experience, however, most people do not have an alternative definition to which they can turn. This book offers such an alternative so that these people can be freed to be faithful.

It may seem odd to some readers for me to argue that we ought to use the word *faith* to mean something different than is usually meant. Isn't this just playing with words? No, I don't think so. *Faith* is a powerful word with centuries of tradition behind it. Many people live their lives seeking a faith of their own and/or trying to create faith in others. Faith is one of the great virtues, so it makes a great deal of difference what that word is used to mean. Is it a virtue to be guillible and dogmatic? Of course not. Yet the word *faith* is often used to mean that. When there is medicine in one bottle and poison in another, we had better be sure the bottles are labeled correctly before deciding which one to take or give to our children. In this book I seek to describe the contents of the bottles clearly, and to get the labels properly marked so that a wise choice can be made.

This book has some important limitations which I wish to acknowledge at the beginning. First, the subject is far too complex to be dealt with completely in any single book. (Actually, of course, faith cannot be completely dealt with in words at all. It must be lived to be understood.) Other books are available that address issues which are omitted or only touched on here. The Pastoral Care Office of the Saints Church has produced one such book, *The Faith Journey* by Luel Hawley Slover and Imogene Goodyear (Herald House, 1982). This work deals with faith development during the various stages of life from childhood to maturity. I certainly recommend it. Another book readers should consider is Paul Tillich's small volume, *The Dynamics of Faith* (Harper and Row, 1957), to which my own work, and indeed most of the best books about faith over the last twenty-five years, are deeply indebted.

A further limitation of this book is my own relative immaturity as a scholar and as a struggler with faith. I am wise enough to have become increasingly aware over the four years since starting this book of how much I do not know about faith. I believe that what is offered here is true and valuable as far as it goes. I offer it with the intention that it will contribute to a continuing discussion about the nature of faith and not as a final work on anything. My hope is that it will enable other, more mature scholars (perhaps even myself in a few years) to do a better, more profound and helpful analysis.

My work on this book has been tremendously important for me, both personally and professionally. I offer it with the sincere hope that the readers will share in my struggle and joy, and that it will help them to make their own faith more whole and mature.

> C. Robert Mesle
> Graceland College
> August 1983

ACKNOWLEDGMENTS

I wish to thank Walter Duty, Christian Education Commissioner for the Saints church, for giving me the opportunity to begin this book during the year that I worked for him. Without his faith in me, and in the value of theology, this book might never have been written. I also want to thank Robert Kent, who wrote the study guide, for his constant encouragement and help as my editor and liaison with the Christian Education Commission. A further, special thanks must go to Clint Woods, my student assistant and friend at Graceland College. He worked long and hard at helping me polish the manuscript. His valuable suggestions ranged from dropping commas to raising basic questions in theology, to pointing out that crabs do not inhabit mountain lakes. The chapter summaries are entirely his work. Yet it is really for his willingness to let me share my frustrations and thought processes out loud that I am grateful.

I also wish to thank my family. My wife, parents, and in-laws undoubtedly suffered much with my spewing of ideas and frustrations. A unique thanks must go to Sarah, my daughter, who played such an important role in teaching me what it means to be grasped. Finally, I owe an apology to Mark, my youngest. You weren't born yet when I wrote the first chapters, Mark. When you are old enough to read this, please forgive me for not having a chapter about you. That can come in another book.

C. Robert Mesle
August 1983

EDITOR'S INTRODUCTION

The intent of this resource has already been outlined in the preface. It seems important, however, to offer further explanation about the nature of *Fire in My Bones* as a *study resource*, including a consideration of the following specific concerns: the part the book plays in a comprehensive Christian education adult study plan, the structure and intent of the study guide, and various study settings.

The Christian Education Adult Study Plan

In 1980 the World Church Christian Education Commission developed a comprehensive, ten-year adult study resource development plan which was approved by the First Presidency. Under the provisions of the plan, the following recommendations relate to a study of this kind.

Some resources should
1. relate to scriptures, theology, and doctrine;
2. address key adult developmental tasks, including religious and intellectual growth;
3. account for a wide range of study methods and study settings;
4. be based soundly on gospel elements;
5. help adults to understand their relationship to the broader Christian community;
6. account for differing perspectives;
7. be written on a variety of reading levels; and
8. be sensitive to disciplines such as historical and theological method and inquiry.

Fire in My Bones addresses this variety of concerns and also relates to the current World Church goal for Christian education in that it may help persons to "know who they are and what the human situation means, grow as children of God rooted in the

Christian community, live in the Spirit of God in every relationship,...and abide in the Christian hope." The study also relates to the World Church Christian Education Commission program objective which calls for "improving the quality of basic theological...understandings held by church members."

Use of the Material

The book is divided into five parts. The first two parts, chapters 1 through 7, apply to readers' concern for understanding the nature of faith.

Chapters in the third part deal with more complex (abstract) ideas. This part of the book serves to stretch readers' minds and cause them to expand some of their assumptions and religious beliefs. This is certainly a concern for Christian education and, again, is consistent with current program goals and objectives.

The fourth part of the book is the most technical. Students would be wise to spend proportionately more time in studying and understanding the implications of the material contained in these chapters. Teachers must be especially sensitive to the needs of students at this point, and be willing to undergo a more intensive process of study, discussion, and consideration of this material. If this is done, students will be able to take time to process this material.

The last part of the book contains three chapters. Chapter 16 includes a reprint of an article on the creative role of doubt in religion and some additional comments and suggestions by the author. Chapter 17 is an allegory depicting different types of theology. These two chapters deal with sensitive issues, and it would be wise to study them only after careful consideration of the preceding material in the book. They present several crucial points which are fundamental to the message of the entire book. Consequently, these should be carefully studied, and may take longer than other chapters. The final chapter ties together key points stated elsewhere. Immediately following this is an activity which will assist students to apply knowledge and understanding gained during the course.

Study and Discussion Questions

Before studying the first chapter, students are encouraged to do the opening activity found on page 19. This will alert students to the complexity of the task of understanding religious language and how it is used.

After reading each chapter, teachers and students may consider together the study and discussion questions found at the end of the chapter. These questions consist of three different kinds: memory, analysis, and evaluation. *Memory* questions primarily ask students to recognize or remember information or facts, state definitions, and review certain parts of the content. *Analysis* questions help students to relate learning to real life situations. This is accomplished by establishing relationships between facts and ideas, making generalizations, comparing, contrasting, and applying understanding from one situation to another. *Evaluation* questions encourage students to determine and use their own standards of judgment. They do so by developing their own opinions and making choices based on comparisons between various elements of the material studied.

Fire in My Bones is intended to make students think first, then apply to their own experiences what they have thought about and learned. Toward this end, a closing activity on page 252 helps students to consider what they have studied and what this can mean in their lives. The author asks students at this point to look to their own behavior and understanding, and where necessary attempt to alter it when dealing with other persons and their faith and beliefs. Presumably, a more disciplined use of such terms by those who have examined and studied them may contribute to better communication and understanding between persons of all "faiths."

Study Settings

Fire in My Bones may be used in a variety of settings, limited only by its length, the time available for study, and its complexity. The book is best studied in settings which allow for full and comprehensive discussion of its key concepts. A twenty-week semester (spring or fall), a small group (either weekly or several nights a week), or individual study are several examples. Individual study of the book is particularly applicable, as it may permit students to take their time in exploring and digesting the material. Study of the book in a group setting, however, will permit an exchange of different responses, ideas, and experiences which may serve to fully process some of the author's varying points of view.

                              Robert E. Kent, editor
                              August 1983

AN OPENING ACTIVITY

This activity can be used as you personally study the book. Complete each activity and then use a dictionary of synonyms to enrich your thought or visit with friends for ideas. When the book is studied in a group setting, divide a large group into several small groups, with each taking a separate word. If the group is small, do the entire activity together.

Procedure
   A. Using the space provided below compile a list of synonyms for each word appearing at the top of the column.

UNFAITHFUL	FAITHFUL	FAITH
_____	_____	_____
_____	_____	_____
_____	_____	_____
_____	_____	_____
_____	_____	_____
_____	_____	_____

   B. Write definitions for the three words in the spaces below.

UNFAITHFUL means _____

FAITHFUL means _____

_____

FAITH means _____

_____

After compiling a list for the word(s), compare and contrast the synonyms with another person or the class. What similarities and differences can be observed? Which synonyms relate more closely to a personal relationship or commitment, such as in trust, loyalty, and honesty? Which synonyms relate more to what one believes or does not believe—a matter of truth or falseness? Which definitions suggest that faith means belief without evidence? What insights did you receive?

Some Observations

This exercise might show several things. One, the word *faith* carries many meanings, even today. If one or even several meanings were taken away and no longer used, there would still be many meanings left for the word *faith*. Two, for some reason negative words like *unfaithful* carry more of the original meaning of faith as commitment or loyalty than does the word *faith*. Essentially then, the original meaning of faith is better preserved in the other forms than in the word *faith* itself.

As you begin to study this book, it will be helpful to recall this activity at various times as one way of illustrating the need to clarify the meaning of the word *faith* and how it is used.

Part I

DEFINITION AND EXAMPLE

Chapter 1
INTRODUCTION: FAITH AS COMMITMENT

Faith is one of the foundations of a meaningful, creative, and purposeful life. It holds our lives together and gives us direction. It is the heart of religion and of life. Without faith, we wander in a spiritual wilderness, a desert dry of the living waters of joy, purpose, meaning, and love.

Faith is wonderfully complex because it is alive and dynamic. It will not hold still for us, neatly separated from the rest of life, to be put into a box and examined at leisure. Living faith is organically related to the rest of life. It does not stand by itself in isolation from other aspects of our thought and feeling. The very act of trying to understand our faith may cause it to change and grow. An honest definition of faith must therefore be a little indefinite at points, acknowledging that the lived experience of faith tends to blur around the edges where it interacts with other experiences, ideas, and feelings.

A natural result of the depth and complexity of the experience of faith is that we frequently do not understand it very well. *Faith* is a word with many meanings. Yet these various meanings do not always illuminate the reality of faith. Indeed, I fear that the most common definitions of faith distort the experience almost beyond recognition. These distortions reflect, and to some extent cause, the distortions of faith which are present in our lives. If we feel strongly that we ought to have faith, but have a mistaken notion of the nature of faith, then the kind of faith for which we are likely to strive will be a distorted one. Paul Tillich, whose insights I seek to interpret in this book, says that faith is among those terms which need healing before they can be used for the healing of persons.*

That healing process can be aided by exploring an understanding of the nature of faith which may assist us in recognizing distortions and directing ourselves toward a solid foundation of faith.

In this exploration, it will be necessary to say something about what faith *is not*. But after saying that faith is definitely *not* something, we may find it necessary to later qualify that claim in order to acknowledge the complexity of our experience. (An example of this, running throughout the book, is the complex relationship between faith and belief.) Necessarily, the definition of faith offered here will conflict with some common definitions. I hope to gradually show, however, that it is a more adequate expression of our deeper intuitions about the nature of the life of faith.

---

*Paul Tillich, *Dynamics of Faith* (New York: Harper and Row, 1957), "Introductory Remarks." The terms *concern, commitment,* and *being grasped,* as synonyms for faith, were popularized by Tillich, but the general approach to faith taken here is that found in the Bible and the bulk of the Christian tradition until the last three centuries.

Definition: Faith as Ultimate Commitment, as Center, and as Courage

The ultimate act of faith is a centering of the whole person—emotions, mind, and will—around a basic commitment or concern. The content of faith is that basic commitment or concern around which the person's life is centered. When faith is no longer an act of the whole person, but is restricted to one part—to emotion alone, to intellect alone, or to will alone—then faith becomes distorted.

Another way of saying this is that faith is a state of "being grasped." This phrase expresses very well my own experience of faith. Certain people, ideas, and values seem to have "gotten a hold on me"; I cannot escape them. They grasp me so that my life is shaped and directed by them. Even if I wanted to ignore them, because of pain or anxiety they cause, I could not. They are centers around which my life revolves.

The prophets Jeremiah and Amos provide powerful expressions of the experience of being grasped. Their lives centered around the prophetic word which they felt called to declare. Though both of them faced great adversity as a result of their prophetic actions, they were grasped by their faith in the God of justice, and by the divine call which had come to them. Even when, in times of anguish, they might have wished to leave this faith behind, they could not. It was the center of their beings. Jeremiah cried, "There seemed to be a fire burning in my heart, imprisoned in my bones. The effort to restrain it wearied me, I could not bear it" (Jeremiah 20:9 JB). Amos declared, "The lion hath roared, who will not fear? the Lord God hath spoken, who can but prophesy?" (Amos 3:8 IV).

Despite the anguish which the grasping of faith may sometimes call us to endure for its sake, the coming of such faith is the occasion for joy. In the words of Jeremiah, "When your words came, I devoured them: your word was my delight and the joy of my heart; for I was called by your name, Yahweh, God of Sabbaoth" (Jeremiah 15:16 JB).

Jeremiah's words suggest that faith brings joy to our lives by giving us a name. In ancient cultures, names were important because they expressed the nature of the person or thing named. To know someone's name was to know something about the nature of that person. Hence, I believe Jeremiah was saying that his faith had made him who he was. It had established his name—his true nature—by the way in which it had grasped him and given his life a center, meaning, and purpose. Faith brings joy by creating our personhood and informing us of who we are.

Of course we do not have only one faith, only one commitment. We are committed to friends and loved ones, to vocations, and to a range of ideas and values. We often feel that these commitments pull us in different directions. The demands of work and family may seem to compete with each other and with our personal desires for enjoyment and self-fulfillment. Our lives threaten to become fragmented, disintegrated.

If our lives are centered around one faith, around one ultimate commitment—one ultimate concern—then our many faiths can become integrated into one whole. Ideally, they will provide mutual support and enrich each other. This bringing together of our many faiths into a centered whole most clearly demonstrates the grasping power of our one ultimate faith. This centering and unifying is an occasion for joy. Such faith creates us as whole persons.

To say clearly just what that one faith is may not be easy. Often, by being the center, it permeates every aspect of life so that to name it separately is difficult. But we know the extent to which we are or are not grasped. When faith grasps us, and pulls our lives together, we rejoice in knowing who we are.

Faith as ultimate commitment is also the ground of courage. The philosopher, Plato, showed that courage is not simply the absence of fear; otherwise, the fool would be the most courageous of persons. Rather courage lies in knowing when we must act in spite of fear—in recognizing what is and is not worthy of risking our lives—and in being willing to undertake that risk. Faith as commitment underlies true courage because it establishes our life priorities and our willingness to risk ourselves in the pursuit of that which we value most highly. Courageous faith can call us into the unknown, into areas of adventure and growth and risk beyond the evidence which we now have. Through faith we discover that we must risk losing our lives in the service of that in which we have found our lives. Courage is one of the hallmarks of faith, but one which is usually perceived in the distorted form of belief without evidence.

Distortions and Misconceptions

Because we are fallible, finite, sinful persons, we will probably experience at least two distortions of faith. First, we may be grasped by something which is *not* of ultimate worth or importance, something which does not deserve our total commitment. We may be ultimately concerned about financial security, recognition, or some good but secondary cause. This is idolatry, the worship of a false god.

Second, we may be grasped by something of ultimate worth, something which deserves our total commitment, but we may not be grasped by it completely. Because our attention is likely to be diverted by all the secondary matters of life, we fail to give ourselves in a way which allows our lives to become centered. The result is a fragmented life.

We cannot overcome either of these distortions completely. Our faith is never fully whole; nor are we able to fully discern the real nature of ultimate value. But faith can grow and mature. This process is part of what it means to be a person moving toward maturity. Nevertheless, we can still see something of the goal toward which we strive: a life fully centered and integrated around an ultimately worthy center which grasps us and gives us meaning and joy.

Within these two basic distortions there are others which continually face us. Since faith is an act or state of centering and integration, distortions of faith occur when faith becomes excessively linked with only one aspect of life. Faith becomes distorted when it becomes excessively emotional, intellectual, or willful to the exclusion of other aspects of life.

For example, the intensity of religious experience can be an important force in grasping us into faith. Yet there is always the danger that we may become "hooked" on the emotional high of the experience itself. Our lives may become directed toward reproducing such emotional experiences for their own sakes. The role of the mind in understanding the experience, and the role of the will in applying it, are denied their rightful places. Not surprisingly, our emotions are also distorted by our eagerness to find total fulfillment in that one kind of experience.

In contrast, we may try to center our lives by a sheer effort of will. We may determine that we will be happy, industrious, or loving whether we want to or not. We coldly calculate the advantages to be gained by such successful self-control. We may even measure the emotional benefits to be received if our emotions will just get out of the way, but such efforts invariably sap our strength of will by cutting off its emotional roots. How can we hope to find joy in life at the expense of our emotions? Somehow our emotions and will must work together in mutual support.

Perhaps the most common misconception of faith regards a distortion of the intellect. Faith is widely defined as belief without or even against the evidence. Many people sense the inadequacy of this definition but are unable to see a clear alternative. I believe very strongly that these people have seen something very important. For one of the most dangerous and prevalent distortions of faith grows out of this misconception.

The relationship between faith and belief is complex. (This relationship will be explored at length in chapter 7; but we need to be alerted now to the dangers of confusing the two.) Faith cannot exist without some beliefs. And yet faith as concern or commitment, as a state of being grasped, is obviously not identical with belief. The distinction is that most beliefs have to do with what is true and false, whereas faith has to do with what is worthy of commitment.

By reducing faith to a matter of belief, the center of life is misplaced in a way which distorts intellect, emotions, and will. In a sense, faith becomes purely intellectual as in a set of answers to a true/false quiz. By insisting that these beliefs be held regardless of contrary evidence, the intellect is crippled and not allowed to do its proper work of examining those answers in the light of reason and experience. Instead, beliefs are maintained by force of emotion and will.

Often the chief emotions sutaining such beliefs are insecurity and pride. We need the security of feeling that we have the right answers to the questions of life. We may also experience pride at having inside knowledge which others may not have. When our beliefs are challenged, our security and pride are threatened, and we become fearful and defensive. The process distorts our entire being. Insofar as faith is reduced to belief without evidence, it ultimately becomes emotional anti-intellectualism.

As we expand the range of our knowledge—of evidence available to us—faith as unfounded belief must shrink before it, hiding in the shadows of our ignorance. Because we will never know all there is to know, this kind of faith will always be able to find some dark corner in which to take refuge. It will, however, become more and more irrelevant and perhaps even destructive to our lives.

To avoid this fate, with its terrible consequences for our lives, religion, and true faith, we must put a proper faith at the center of our lives where it can hold together the many facets of our reason and experience. With a healthy, intelligent faith at the center, our many secondary faiths may be put into proper perspective and given fruitful expression through the one faith by which we are ultimately grasped.

One further distortion of faith requires some comment here. There is a strong tendency to think of faith as a kind of magic. We sometimes speak as if simply believing something strongly enough will make it come true. People who are deeply committed to a cause may move some very large mountains; but they do so only by hard work and tireless dedication, not by wishing.

There is a fundamental distinction between faith (or religion) and magic. Magic seeks to control or manipulate the world and the gods, to bend them to the magician's will. Faith, in direct contrast, seeks to bend our will to that of God—whatever that may be. Thus faith is never magic. It does not move the mountain by "believing real hard." Faith moves mountains when faithful people are willing to carry the mountain on their backs to take it where it needs to be.

Plan of the Book

In this text faith is addressed primarily in a theological context, with the concern that it illuminate the meaning of specifically Christian faith. Consequently, there is naturally a desire to move directly to a discussion of faith in God, Christ, the scriptures, and the church. But this will be resisted for two reasons.

First, faith is not something which applies only to part of life. Although we most commonly use the term in conjunction with so-called religious or doctrinal beliefs, faith deals with every major aspect of life. Second, when we discuss faith with regard to the highly emotional and sensitive issues of religious belief, there is a strong tendency to confuse the discussion of faith with the content of particular beliefs. Our understanding of the nature of faith in general will naturally have important implications for our understanding of what it means to have faith in God or faith in the church, but we should avoid confusing them more than necessary. This is a book about the nature of faith, not about the nature of God.

Consequently, the meaning of faith will be explored in the first two parts of the book without specific reference to doctrinal issues. Instead, the nature of faith as it relates to the experiences of hope, trust, love, and belief will be clarified. After this groundwork is laid then this view of faith will be applied to the meaning of specifically Christian faith.

Summary
1. Faith, as organically related to the rest of life, is alive and dynamic. It does not stand apart from the rest of our experience in order for us to study it. Our definitions of faith will, therefore, be indefinite at points.
2. The many common misunderstandings of the faith experience must be dealt with before we can fully appreciate that experience.
3. The ultimate act of faith is the centering of the whole person—emotions, mind, and will—around a basic commitment or concern. Faith becomes distorted when this integration is destroyed by one element of our personality assuming a dominant position.
4. The content of faith is that basic commitment or

concern around which a person's life is centered.
5. The faith experience is the experience of being grasped by, for example, a person, idea, or value, which demands recognition as a center around which our lives turn.
6. Faith brings joy by giving us our true nature and telling us who we are.
7. Our many secondary faiths ideally become integrated with and enriched by one another in their relationship with the one ultimate faith commitment around which our lives are centered. This integration is made by the grasping power of our one basic, ultimate faith.
8. Courage, the willingness to risk ourselves in the pursuit of that which we value most highly, is a hallmark of faith.
9. Two of the most common distortions of faith are the experience of being ultimately grasped by something which is not worthy of our ultimate faith commitment, and the experience of not being grasped totally by that which deserves our ultimate faith commitment.
10. Our goal is a life fully centered and integrated around an ultimately worthy center which grasps us and gives us meaning and joy.
11. Perhaps the most common misconception of faith is its definition as belief without or against evidence. While there can be no faith without beliefs, the two are not identical. Beliefs deal with factual truth or falsity; faith deals with what is worthy of commitment.
12. When faith is seen as belief without evidence, it ends up as emotional anti-intellectualism bolstered by insecurity and pride. This faith has dangerous consequences for our lives.
13. Faith sometimes is distorted to mean magic which seeks to bend the will of the "powers that be" to the magician's will; faith seeks to bend

our will to that of God.
14. Faith deals with every aspect of our lives.

Study and Discussion Questions
1. The author states that faith is alive and dynamic, and that it is not isolated from the rest of life. Is this consistent with your view of faith? Why or why not?
2. If "the very act of trying to understand our faith may cause it to grow and change" is true, how can this be a positive factor in faith development? How comfortable are you with a definition of faith which is "indefinite at points"? How is this like other experiences in life, in terms of distortions and potential misunderstandings? How does this serve to underline the author's belief about faith's integration in life?
3. What are your reactions to the distinction between faith as a "centering act"and the "content" as a "commitment of ultimate concern"? How does this help you in clarifying your understanding of faith?
4. Recall an occasion when you have felt pulled in different directions by competing interests, concerns, and commitments. In what ways would your life be more joyful if these competing factors were grounded by a faith which unifies them? (One way of looking at this would be to say that your commitments to friends and family do not compete with your commitment to—your faith in—God; rather they are reflections of your ultimate commitment. They are grounded in, and united with, that one true faith.) How does this insight clarify your view toward your current commitments?
5. Starting on page 26, the author explores a variety of distortions and misconceptions about faith. Reflect on your own views of faith and identify which of these may have characterized

your own understanding. When have you viewed faith primarily in either emotional or intellectual terms? When as an exercise of supreme willpower? How might this have been a distortion of the one true faith which encompasses all three aspects of life? Similarly, how has your faith been a kind of security blanket or a matter of personal pride? In what ways does this view still seem adequate or inadequate?

6. What are your impressions of the suggestion that if faith is equivalent to beliefs, when beliefs prove to be false, one's faith is shaken? In what ways, then, is it important to separate faith from belief (pages 27-29)? Why is this separation necessary in a world of ever-growing and ever-increasing knowledge?

7. Recall an instance when you felt your faith faltering because of a changed belief. What was the particular belief? How did you overcome this crisis? In what ways does your current faith accommodate changing beliefs?

8. When have you used your faith as magic by trying to manipulate God or a person? What elements of the experience can you recall? Understanding faith as active commitment, how would you relive that experience, if you could?

9. If true faith is the experience of being grasped by something of ultimate importance, what is the character of your true faith? By what are you currently grasped? How is this ultimate concern the center of your life? How do all your other concerns relate to it?

10. Reflect on the material in the chapter and state one important new insight you have received.

_____

_____

_____

Chapter 2
FAITH AS BEING GRASPED: MY EXPERIENCE WITH SARAH

Introduction

In this chapter I have attempted to develop at length one example of my own experience with faith. In keeping with the strategy outlined at the end of chapter 1, this example is not related to a doctrinal issue, but to a personal relationship. I have chosen to do this for several reasons.

First, this is an appeal to a virtually universal experience. It is a rare and unfortunate person who is not deeply grasped by the worth of some other person. Second, this example is not controversial. We are not likely to be sidetracked into secondary disagreements. Third, it can help to clarify the ways in which faith is distinct from, and yet related to, the affiliated experiences of belief, hope, and trust. Finally, the development of this example at length will provide a touchstone to which readers can refer in trying to understand more difficult issues later in the book. By asking "What did the author mean in regard to Sarah?" or even "How does this compare with my relationship to persons by whom I am grasped?" it may be possible to interpret the meaning of this example in other cases.

Faith That "Sarah Matters"

When I first held my newborn daughter Sarah, something important happened to me which has helped me to understand the nature of faith. No words can fully capture what I experienced. (This is an important fact to recognize in itself.) Some words or phrases can, however, *point to* the experience. To begin with, I would say that I was grasped by Sarah. In the first moment of holding her I felt that her life was somehow reaching out to grasp mine in a way that transformed and redirected me. I became concerned about and committed to her. Indeed, I could say that I became ultimately concerned and ultimately committed. I experienced Sarah's infinite and unconditional worth; or in the words I used to express this to friends, *Sarah matters.*

A basic distinction must be made between judgments of fact and judgments of value, even though the two are interrelated and the distinction is often difficult to describe. There is a difference between knowing what a painting looks like and deciding whether or not you like it, or between determining that a person stole something and judging whether the theft was immoral. There is certainly a difference between knowing all about someone and falling in love with that person. In each of these cases, the former is a judgment of fact, the latter a judgment of value; the former has an important, perhaps essential, impact on the latter, but the two remain distinct. In each case, two persons with the same set of facts may arrive at different judgments about values.

My claim that Sarah matters is not like the claims that 2 + 2 = 4, or that water is a liquid. These are statements of objective facts which in no way depend on personal feelings or values. They are either true or false; and the decision about their truth or falsehood must not be influenced by personal feelings. My claim that Sarah matters, however, is not true or false in the way that these two statements are. I must turn to my *feelings* to decide her mattering, for the actual question is: Do I *feel* that she matters? As with all judgments of value, this one is related to judgments of fact, but is not identical with them.

The crucial distinction between these two kinds of judgments is often confused because the word *belief* is used in both cases. "I believe she is honest." "I believe in honesty." Faith is a form of value judgment related to *facts*, but ultimately dependent on *feelings*. As such, it cannot tell us what is factually true or false.

Consequently I cannot prove that Sarah matters— I can only declare my feeling that she does. Nor can you decide by weighing the evidence or arguments that Sarah or any other person will or will not matter to you. The mattering of persons is something which is discovered as they are encountered. Faith is thus not logically or factually true or false.

Still we can and do speak of the truth of faith. When we ask if my faith in Sarah is true, we are asking about the quality and depth of my commitment. We are asking if I am truly concerned about and committed to Sarah. Faith is true in the way that love is true, not in the way that factual beliefs are true. Faith is true or false in the sense of being alive or dead, loyal or disloyal, whole or broken. I know that my faith in Sarah is powerfully alive because I feel it grasping me.

Yet my faith in Sarah is not purely self-contained. There is something about Sarah and about my experience as a human being in the world with other persons which gives birth to this faith. Sarah does not matter in a vacuum. She matters to me in the context of a whole world of facts, beliefs, expectations, and values. We might even wish to affirm, in some contexts, that her mattering is grounded in the very structures of human experience. But, finally, in such matters, "The heart has reasons reason knows not of."*

Faith and Belief

Although my faith in Sarah's mattering is not to be identified with any particular belief, trust, or hope that I have in regard to her life, these will arise as I live out my commitment to her. Because I am ultimately grasped by the value of Sarah's life, I will see possibilities in her and make sacrifices for her that others would not. Because I care about her I will want her to be trustworthy; that will lead me to trust her. Because my life is involved in hers, I will be filled with hopes for the wonderful things she might accomplish, and I will strive to help her achieve them. Out of my being grasped by Sarah, there will arise acts of belief, trust, and hope.

Sarah's ability to believe, trust, hope, love, and experience faith will largely be a product of the belief, trust, hope, love, and faith which others invest in her. The quality and quantity of love which persons are able to give are directly related to the quality and quantity of love which they receive. This is true of the other gifts named above as well. With the support of people who sense her worth and dignity, Sarah can discover and nurture all the wonderful possibilities already growing within her. Her unconditional worth as a person can flower into concrete actions which are of value to others.

As Sarah and I go through life, however, some of

---

*Blaise Pascal (1632-62), *Penses*, IV, 277.

my beliefs about her will be proved false. Some acts of trust may be betrayed. Some hopes will not be fulfilled. In some cases, these things will occur because Sarah's interests will be different from mine; in others, she may fail to achieve her own goals. At times she may fail because my ultimate commitment to her may have become confused with specific beliefs about what she is or ought to be. I may fail to see her as she really is or I may try to shape her in my own wishful image. My basically good faith in her will become, in that situation, destructive. I must then step back and admit that I confused faith with belief, concern with understanding.

At times Sarah will simply fail. She will be weak and sinful (as well as great and wonderful) like all persons. Whether in large things or small, she will sometimes lie, and perhaps even steal or hurt others intentionally. Like all of us, she will not be perfect.

This difficult realization has reinforced my view that faith must not be identified with specific beliefs about the object of faith. If I were to confuse faith with belief, trust, or hope, then I might become very confused about Sarah's mattering when these expectations prove mistaken. I might even accuse Sarah of having destroyed my faith in her. Such confusion could be very destructive even if I really continued to care about Sarah; and the fault would be mine, not hers.

Even if I did not make that mistake, even if I understood in my mind that Sarah matters unconditionally, I, too, am weak and sinful. If Sarah were to hurt me badly enough for long enough, it is humanly possible that I might cease to care about her. I might lose my faith. If that happened it would be a terrible tragedy.

Perhaps two illustrations will help to clarify the relationship between belief and faith.

My wife and I love classical violin music. If Sarah decides someday that she would like to play the violin, we would gladly encourage her. Now suppose that her instructor tells us that Sarah has the ability to become a concert performer. Our belief that Sarah can become a great violin virtuoso combined with our love for music and for her could become the foundation for a basic life of faith, a commitment toward making this dream come true. We might say, loosely, that we have faith that Sarah will become a concert violinist.

Suppose, however, that Sarah is also told that she could become a fine painter. There are now competing beliefs and interests. Our belief that Sarah could become a great virtuoso remains. But our faith, our commitment to a way of life, may change. The *truth* of a belief does not automatically make it an *occasion* for faith.

In contrast, suppose that for some reason we discover that Sarah cannot become an accomplished violin player. Lack of talent, disease, injury, or other circumstances may intervene. Although our faith might lead us to work toward a dream through great adversity, it will not change the facts. A severed hand will not be restored by our commitment to Sarah's future. In this case, the falsehood of a belief forces us to abandon a faith commitment.

If our faith in Sarah and her future have been strictly identified with that particular belief about her, then we and she may feel that our faith in her and her future has been destroyed. We, and she, could easily collapse into a deep despair about life.

If we dig deeply, however, we may discover that our more fundamental faith did not depend on that belief for its existence. Our more fundamental faith was and is in Sarah herself, in her worth, and in the importance of developing her potential as far as possible. The evidence has forced a change of belief about Sarah, and hence a redirection of our ultima' commitment to the beauty of her life. Only the p/ ticular expression of the more ultimate faith] been displaced. Our faith in Sarah will lead us t(

examine the ways in which Sarah's life can develop to its fullest potential. A belief has been disproved; particular commitment based on that belief has been abandoned. Yet our faith in Sarah remains alive and powerful.

Let me offer a second imaginary—rather fanciful—illustration.

Although I was in the hospital delivery room at the time of Sarah's birth, I did not actually hold her until later. Despite the excitement of delivery, it was in first holding Sarah that I was so powerfully grasped by her as an individual. What would have happened if, after this first powerful experience of being grasped by an infant girl, the nurse had come in with a red face, explained that she had given me the wrong infant, and exchanged babies with me? How might I have felt? I would like to offer four possible responses. First, the original baby could have passed out of my life to be forgotten except as an unusual incident. Second, I might have become disillusioned with parental love. "If I feel that way about any kid they happen to hand me," I might have reasoned, "what is this love but a rush of hormones?" I might have been suspicious of such feelings all my life, thinking that I had some dark, secret knowledge which others did not have. I could have become a parental cynic. Third, I might have refused to shift my faith, and spent my whole life neurotically insisting that the first child was really Sarah, regardless of all evidence to the contrary. Fourth, I might have realized that my experience of being grasped by one child revealed the possibility of being grasped by all children, by all persons. Thus, my experience with the first child could have expanded to include Sarah. Though my commitment to Sarah would have grown in depth and richness over the years, so that it became unique, I could always have remembered that her power to grasp me is shared by all persons to whom I will open myself.

Both of these illustrations suggest some of the different ways in which we may respond to a radical change of beliefs about the object of our faith. Beliefs and faith are closely related but are not identical. Faith commitments can change while beliefs remain the same. Or a change in beliefs may cause us to reexamine our faith so that we discover that its deepest foundation is independent of the particular beliefs in question.

In summary, there are both *relative* and *absolute* threats to faith. The relative threat is that the specific beliefs, trusts, and hopes arising out of and supporting our faith will prove false. This threat is relative because a strong faith, properly understood, may be able to survive this and express itself in new, richer, and more adequate beliefs and hopes. The absolute threat is that we may cease to be grasped. Faith itself may die.

Many times I will feel that I can do nothing for Sarah, that she will be on her own. At times I will not know what to believe or even what to hope. At times I will not know whether I should invest my trust in her. But in all of these times, I must make it clear to her that I am still grasped by my basic faith that Sarah matters.

The discovery that faith can continue to live when fundamental beliefs are found to be mistaken or inadequate is one which requires much courage, but which yields great possibilities for growth. To refuse to let beliefs and hopes change is to deny the real, inherent worth of the object of faith and to insist that if this object is not just what we want it to be, we will not care about it. Such faith strangles itself slowly. We experience pain when children grow and make their own decisions about what they will do and be, especially when those decisions run counter to our own hopes. But we must allow this if we really care. In the same way, we must allow ourselves and our faith to grow and change, even when that growth is painful.

This brings us to the last major point I wish to make about faith in this chapter.

Faith Which Points Beyond

In my more profound moments, I feel that Sarah's mattering points beyond Sarah herself to the mattering of all persons. I hope this is so, because the real question is not whether Sarah's life proves that other people matter, but whether my encounter with Sarah has helped to disclose and strengthen within me a fundamental concern for and commitment to all people. This is not something I can prove about other people. Rather, it is a question I must ask myself: Do I have faith in, am I ultimately grasped by, the worth of all persons?

I definitely care, emotionally, more about Sarah than about children who are not my own. But Sarah's life has done something important to my feelings about other people. When I think of hungry or frightened children now, I am likely, unintentionally, to see Sarah in their place. The face in the picture or in my mind's eye becomes Sarah's face. When I think of their parents, I become them. Even adults can wear Sarah's face. When this happens, I discover that in that moment I am grasped by that other person as by my own child.

There is a mystery here which I cannot capture in words, but which lies at the very heart of faith.

In the experience of faith we are usually grasped by some specific person, thing, or idea. We become committed to and concerned about that person, thing, or idea. To that extent, we set the object of our faith above other such objects. If we allow ourselves to stop there, our faith becomes idolatry. We become narrow and exclusive. We will feel threatened by claims for the worth of other objects of faith.

If the object of our faith is truly worthy of our ultimate concern, we will discover, however, that its worth lies partly in its power to participate in and point toward something larger and deeper. That is the case with Sarah. I am discovering that part of her worth and significance lies in her power to nurture, expand, and direct my faith in her toward faith in the ultimate worth of all persons.

To support my interpretation of faith, I would appeal to the common experience of how we evaluate the maturity of persons. If a child is selfish, insisting on receiving all the attention and being valued over all other people and concerns, we see that as a mark of immaturity and lack of understanding. Similarly, if parents are so narrowly committed to their own child that they cannot deal fairly with other children and adults involved with their child, we again see that as a mark of immaturity and lack of understanding in the parents. We do not consider it a virtue for parents to be so wrapped up in their children that they cannot see the rights and worth of other persons. These are cases where legitimate concern for self and others has become distorted into idolatry. Faith has become demonic.

It seems essential for us, however, that our most basic faith have a focal point in some specific person, object, or idea. We cannot grasp, either emotionally or intellectually, the whole of reality, the whole realm of value. Therefore we must find that worth in some particular thing or person or idea which reveals ultimate value to us. True faith, I am convinced, means commitment and concern. An object worthy of such concern directs us beyond itself toward something larger and deeper which it reflects, and in which it participates.

To be ultimately committed to Sarah is to be committed to someone real, concrete, and particular. There is nothing abstract or general about Sarah. Despite that—or perhaps because of that—Sarah is wonderfully able to act as a symbol for all persons. Her mattering is what reveals or discloses to me, as well as nurtures within me, my faith in the worth of all persons. However weak and inadequate my own faith may be, I believe that this experience with Sarah has helped reveal to me the true nature of faith and the sign of an object worthy of faith.

Summary
1. Faith as a personal relationship is universal. It is related to, but distinct from, experiences of belief, hope, and trust.
2. Faith as personal relationship is indescribable but can be pointed to symbolically.
3. Faith as personal relationship consists in being grasped by another. The other, who becomes the object of concern and commitment, is recognized as one who matters.
4. Faith is true in the way that love is true. The truth of faith is a matter which deals with the quality and depth of commitment, not objective fact.
5. The mattering of persons is discovered in personal encounter with them within a context of a world of facts, beliefs, expectations, and values.
6. The quality and quantity of belief, love, trust, hope, and faith which people are able to give are directly related to the quality and quantity of these gifts they receive.
7. Faith must not be confused with specific beliefs, expectations, or desires about the person who matters.
8. Courage is required in order to enable faith to grow. This courage accepts the pain involved in the loss of specific beliefs, expectations, or trust by acknowledging a deeper foundation in the mattering of a person.
9. Faith as personal relationship points beyond the individual by which we are grasped and participates in a deeper, broader reality: the mattering of all person. The object by which we are grasped, if truly worthy of our ultimate concern

and commitment, will serve as a focal point for a larger realm of ultimacy.

Study and Discussion Questions

1. The author distinguishes between two different kinds of statements or judgments: those related to *facts* and those related to *feelings*. Since one word—belief—is used to refer to both kinds of judgments, many become confused about what is really meant. Write down three statements of your belief. Which ones are statements of fact (true or false) and can be proven? Which ones are statements about how you feel (someone or something matters)?

    A. _____

    _____

    _____

    B. _____

    _____

    _____

    C. _____

    _____

    _____

2. Recall a time when someone betrayed your trust. How did this change your belief about that person? Did that person actually cease to matter to you from then on? Why or why not?
3. Reread the two illustrations used to distinguish faith from belief: Sarah as a potential violin virtuoso and her father's experience on first

holding her. How are they different? How are they similar? What additional illustrations of the distinction between faith and belief can you provide from your own experience?

4. The author suggests that competing beliefs need not weaken personal faith. What are the implications of this for commitments which expose you to competing and even conflicting beliefs, such as in the church, the community, and your family? How might this understanding serve to strengthen your commitments to other persons, like the commitment of Sarah's parents to her?

5. Faith may remain strong, even when specific beliefs change. Can you recall, on the other hand, an instance when a change in belief actually changed your faith? In what way did your faith die? How was it redirected? How was it strengthened? How did this occur?

6. The experience of Sarah's father with her served to point toward the worth and mattering of all persons. In this way, Sarah serves as a symbolic object of faith. What are the symbols or objects of your faith? How do these objects or symbols point toward the worth of others? If they do not, why not? Why may you need to re-evaluate what is symbolized by the objects of your faith? How have they possibly become confused with the greater reality toward which they point? How can you keep from falling into the trap of idolatry, where you place one object above all others?

7. What new insights have you received? How might these help in your growing understanding of faith?

_____

_____

Part II

WORKING OUT SOME DETAILS

Chapter 3
THE KALEIDOSCOPE OF FAITH*

As you turn a kaleidoscope and look toward the light, a blaze of previously unseen colors and patterns surges into view. Another turn and the red, yellow, and blue snowflakes become orange suns blazing in a purple sky. The beauty of a good kaleidoscope is that it provides an almost inexhaustible variety of visions without changing the essential elements of which it is made. Indeed, it is almost impossible to prevent the transformations. A slight twist or movement can produce a metamorphosis—and reveal new beauty, new possibilities, and new perspectives.

The experience of faith is also kaleidoscopic. We

---
*This chapter appeared in an earlier form on pages 15-26 of *The Faith Journey* by Luel Hawley Slover and Imogene Goodyear (Herald House, 1982).

cannot put faith into a cardboard tube pointed at a light and twirl it around, but we can turn it over in our mind's eye and hold it under the light of careful reflection. As we attend to the nature of faith we will discover that, like the kaleidoscope, it can reveal myriad facets without changing its essential nature. Hold it in our minds this way and we see an intricate pattern of beliefs. Turn it slightly in that direction and the beliefs disappear completely, leaving only a splash of brightly colored emotion. Yet another turn and we see a path to be followed on a journey or perhaps a journey itself. Held in one light, faith looks like a noun, as fixed and stable as a rock. In another light it moves and shimmers like a verb bursting into action. When the mind turns the kaleidoscope of faith just so, and shines its critical reflection on it very brightly, the elements may seem for a moment to disappear completely, leaving only mystery. Paradoxically, it may be that when this happens faith is revealed to us most truly.

In this book we will examine some of the facets and patterns which are involved in the complex experience we call faith. This chapter offers some reflections on the struggle to examine the basic nature of faith. Through the image of the kaleidoscope of faith we can step back and review the problem and our efforts from a fresh perspective. Thus this chapter is at once a preview of the problem and a suggestion for some tentative conclusions.

Problems in Understanding Faith

What problems confront us in our quest to understand the nature of faith? What approaches to faith are helpful? Let us begin our review by returning to the symbol of the kaleidoscope.

When we look into the kaleidoscope, we see many different colors and patterns at different times. Yet all of those many patterns are created out of the same basic "stuff." If we were very young children seeing all of this for the first time, we might easily misunderstand what is happening. We might not realize, for example, that the patterns we saw were all made out of the same elements. This could easily lead us to think that each of the patterns we saw was distinct and separate, rather than being the product of a complex mixing of elements common to many patterns. We would probably not realize how the patterns flowed into each other and arose out of each other. These errors could create a natural assumption that the patterns we had seen in our two or three turns with the kaleidoscope were the only patterns to be seen. How could we possibly imagine the endless variety waiting to be revealed to the persistent viewer!

What would happen if we—still as children—tried to name the patterns we had seen? Would our names help or hinder a person trying to understand the basic nature of the kaleidoscope? While our names might be of some help, they would be confusing in at least three different ways.

First, we would have no separate name for the basic stuff out of which the patterns and colors arise. It would be like knowing specific words without having the concepts of "word" or "letter." (Children, of course, go through exactly this problem.) Or we might say that it would be like having the names red, yellow, blue, and round, square, oval, while lacking the concepts or words "color" and "shape." Second, we would be giving names to patterns which we thought were fixed and stable. Thus our names might not allow for the ways in which the patterns could change slightly or greatly, or flow into completely new patterns when the kaleidoscope was turned. Nor would our names allow for the uniqueness of each new pattern. Finally, thinking that the patterns we had seen and named were the only patterns, we might not believe—and would certainly be suspicious of—any person who claimed to have seen a different pattern. We would not even have a name with which to talk about it. For these reasons our names for the patterns may not really help us to understand the basic *nature* of the kaleidoscope.

A discussion of the nature of faith is likely to run into similar difficulties. We have usually failed to recognize faith's kaleidoscopic nature. And obviously, the discussion of faith is both vastly more complex and more important.

We have experiences which we call belief, trust, hope, commitment, love, meaning, and so on. These experiences are like the patterns in the kaleidoscope. They are distinguishable from each other at times, but they are not ultimately separate or unrelated. With a little turn of our vision, one can look very much like another. For example, when parents decide to give a child new privileges, is that an expression of trust, hope, belief, or caring? All of these? Something else? Is it an act of faith? If so, how is it different from or related to these others? On the whole, the discussion can be very confusing.

To help clarify this confusion of names and experiences, we can look at three problems in discussing faith which are similar to those of the children naming the patterns in the kaleidoscope. First, we usually fail to see a common basic nature or experience out of which the many experiences arise. We do have a name which sometimes points to such a basic experience, faith, but we do not always use it that way. For example, when asking about the basic nature of faith, one person may fix on the idea of *belief* and say that is *faith*, while another may emphasize *trust*, and yet another can speak only of *hope*. These descriptions recognize important *dimensions* of faith, but not the basic *nature* of faith. Second, we tend to treat these experiences as if they were entirely separate. Since they actually arise out of something common to them all, however, they very naturally flow and merge so that it can be difficult to tell them apart. We neglect the uniqueness of each new experience. Finally, we tend to use these words very restrictively. If people speak of experiences of faith different from those we have had, we are confused and frustrated. We may be suspicious of them. Or we may feel perplexed, troubled, and even guilty if we have not experienced faith in the same way they have.

Progress can be made toward removing some of this confusion by looking for some more basic understanding of the broad nature of faith as such. An understanding of this type should help us to see more clearly the relationships and diversities which exist between the many forms and expressions of faith.

Given the complexity and fluid nature of the experience of faith, there can never be a fully adequate analysis of it. Human life cannot be captured in a box of words and made to stand still while we map its every feature. Yet that ultimate limitation does not remove either the responsibility or the desire to search for more adequate insights than we now have. We have, therefore, tried to come to some understanding of the basic nature of faith.

Toward an Understanding of Faith

Faith is a form of *experience*. This might seem rather obvious, but that does not make it less important or even easy to understand. (We often miss things precisely because they are obvious.) To say that faith is a form of experience is to distinguish it from the *content* of any *particular* experience of faith. Remember that we are seeking to understand the basic nature of faith itself, and not to learn about the many specific beliefs individuals or groups may have. Two people, for example, may have very different hopes. That is, the content of their experience of hope may be very different. But they both *experience* hope. Two people may have exactly opposite beliefs, but they both experience belief. It may be true that we never experience belief or hope or any form of faith without some specific content which gives shape and character to the experience; but we are looking for the common nature shared by all of these experiences of faith.

The next question seems to be: what kind of an experience is faith? One of the facts of life which we must often confront is that language can never fully convey experience. I cannot tell you what peppermint tastes like, nor can you tell me what yellow looks like. Fortunately, however, we share enough experiences in common that some communication is possible.

We have already noted how especially confusing the language of faith can be. If I say that faith is like trust, or hope, or caring, can I finally make my meaning clear? Perhaps not, but we must try. In order to avoid some of these language problems, a term not usually associated with the discussion of faith was introduced. This was chosen to avoid bringing in unwanted preconceptions which other words carry with them. Yet the word does provide a foundation upon which we can build by referring to those other, more common, words, and saying that faith is "like" trust in this way and hope in that way.

The term proposed was one suggested by Paul Tillich who says that faith for him is an experience of "being grasped." After all of our reflection is over, we may still be asking "what does it mean to be grasped?" A preliminary comment may help. When we grasp or get a hold on something, it cannot get away from us. At least it cannot get away if we grasp it firmly. We may grasp it strongly or weakly. If we are grasping a fish, for example, it will be slippery and wiggle; if we do not grasp it very tightly it will escape us. If we know how, we may grasp the fish so that no amount of squirming will enable it to escape.

The experience of faith is the experience of being grasped by someone or something. We may be grasped powerfully or weakly. If we are grasped powerfully, we cannot get away, regardless of how hard we try. But faith is quite different from a grasping hand. The hand is not part of what it grasps (the fish, for example). The experience of faith, however, is part of us. Faith is an experience which shapes personal being. If it grasps us powerfully, it may be a central element in determining who we are. If faith grasps us at the center of our lives, we live and move and think and feel and act in a way which reflects that faith.

Saying that we are grasped, however, does not yet tell us enough about the experience of faith. By what are we grasped? The kaleidoscope image of faith points at the fact that there can be an almost infinite number of specific beliefs or hopes or commitments by which we may be grasped. That is, faith may have a wide variety of contents, or take innumerable forms. Yet it is not necessary or adequate to go directly from the question "What grasps us in the experience of faith?" to these many different answers. At least one answer is basic to all experiences of faith.

Faith is the experience of being grasped by the feeling that something or someone matters. Ultimate faith is to be grasped fully, totally, by the sense that something or someone matters ultimately. Faith is ultimate concern, as Tillich says. For example, my family matters to me in a way which is central to my life. My struggle to understand also matters in a powerful, though different, way. I am in the grasp of these and other concerns which matter to me, and from which I could not escape even if I wanted to. The fish might squirm out of a grasping hand, but I cannot escape the grasp of these things which matter. Their "mattering" is part of who I am.

The test of such a view is whether or not it helps us to make sense out of the many ways in which we experience faith. We can be grasped by trust in a person, by hope in a future, by commitment to an institution, or by belief that there is a loving God. These trusts, hopes, concerns, and beliefs give our experience of faith content, shape, and structure. They are the patterns and colors in the kaleidoscope of faith. They are the specific answers we give to questions about the content of our faith. Yet are we not grasped by them precisely because they matter to us a great deal?

The scriptures are full of testimonies of faith as the experience of being grasped by the ultimate mattering of God, of Christ, or of the church. It may be helpful to recall the testimonies of Jeremiah and Amos which were referred to in chapter 1.

When your words came, I devoured them: your word was my delight and the joy of my heart; for I was called by your name, Yahweh, God of Sabbaoth.—Jeremiah 15:16 JB

There seemed to be a fire burning in my heart, imprisoned in my bones. The effort to restrain it wearied me, I could not bear it.—Jeremiah 20:9 JB

The lion hath roared, who will not fear? the Lord God hath spoken, who can but prophesy?—Amos 3:8 IV

These testimonies speak of the power of the Word of God to grasp the lives of people. Such testimonies abound in the scriptures. They are often filled with the joy of discovering a new meaning and direction in life. To discover something which matters ultimately, by which one is supremely grasped, to have a fire burning in one's bones, is to acquire a new direction for one's existence. It is to be able to declare, "Now I know who I am and where I am going!" How many of us have sought for such a center for our lives!

Although most people have a multitude of things which matter to them, they find that they hunger for that one thing which will grasp them with the overwhelming sense that *this* matters ultimately. *This* has become the center of life around which all else moves and, in light of which, thought, feeling, and action arise. A beautiful expression of such a centered life is found in the familiar biblical words of Ruth to her mother-in-law:

Entreat me not to leave you or to return from following you; for where you go I will go, and where you lodge I will lodge; your people shall be my people, and your God my God; where you die I will die, and there will I be buried.—Ruth 1:16, 17 RSV

The contrast between life lived with and without such a center is illustrated in the story of Martha and Mary in Luke 10:38-41. Martha was embroiled with the necessary but distracting details of serving food while her sister, Mary, sat at Jesus' feet and listened to his teaching. In response to Martha's complaint, Jesus answered,

Martha, Martha, you are anxious and troubled about many things; one thing is needful. Mary has chosen the good portion, which shall not be taken away from her.—Luke 10:41, 42 RSV (42, 43 IV)

To have such an ultimate faith at the center of one's life does not mean that other elements automatically lose all their importance. It means, rather, that the importance of those elements is measured by and expressed in the ultimate concern. In some cases, many things may become far more important than they were before because they can now be experienced as ways of acting out or supporting the central commitment. Many people have found this to be true with their religious faith. Lives that were falling apart for lack of a unifying center, for lack of something that really mattered, have found new wholeness. Family, work, and even recreation have come to be part of unified lives lived out of a central faith in Christ.

Obviously, however, human existence is never totally centered in one faith commitment. We are continually torn by competing concerns and beliefs and desires. Our lives are not fully centered or unified. They are not going in just one direction. It is just this lack of wholeness which creates within us that hunger for a faith that can give a center to life.

We hunger for lives on fire with a unifying commitment.

Part of the reason for our lack of wholeness, however, is that we want faith to be too easy. We want to think that we know the two or three patterns in the kaleidoscope of faith which are final and "true." We want to think of these few patterns as fixed and settled. But life changes. We change. We are not grasped by the same things at different stages of our lives. Hence faith changes, too. To attempt to keep faith fixed is to refuse to grow. This means that it may be helpful at times to think of faith as a process or a journey through which we move and in which we pause at different stages.

Living Faith

The painfulness with which such change may be experienced is expressed powerfully by the prophet Malachi. Malachi lived in a time when the people of Israel were challenging inherited ideas. They had been told that God would protect and reward the faithful—the "piety-prosperity" theory. Yet their experience conflicted with this, and so they were angry. The prophet records their frustrations.

> You have wearied the Lord with your words. Yet you say, "How have we wearied him?" By saying, "Everyone who does evil is good in the sight of the Lord, and he delights in them." Or by asking, "Where is the God of justice?"—Malachi 2:17 RSV

Malachi's response to this challenge is very suggestive.

> The Lord whom ye seek, shall suddenly come to his temple, even the messenger of the covenant, whom ye delight in; behold, he shall come, saith the Lord of hosts. But who may abide the day of his coming? and who shall stand when he appeareth? for he is like a refiner's fire.—Malachi 3:1, 2 IV

Whenever we become aware of the inadequacies of our old ideas and commitments, we face the terrible prospect that we might be called upon to grow into new understandings and new commitments. In many different ways the God whom we seek may be far larger and more demanding than we had expected. If we ask seriously for a God of justice, we may suddenly find our own lack of justice disclosed to us. Along with that painful insight may come a call to a new kind of life dedicated to the establishment of justice for others rather than ourselves. If we point out the inadequacies in the theologies of those about us, we may suddenly be confronted with the shallowness of our own understandings of God and the world. These and other forms of growth may come to us as painfully as immersion in the "refiner's fire." The process of growth in faith is not an easy one. The fire which burns within our bones does not give us unity of life without demanding that we commit our lives to its fire. This is why faith often expresses itself in courage. Those who would save their lives must lose them.

Faith is indeed a kaleidoscopic experience. Turned this way we see it as belief or trust. Turned that way it appears as commitment or love. When we make the mistake of identifying faith with a specific content, faith looks like something we can capture, examine, understand, and even hand on to others. But real faith is not finally like this. Faith, like all real experiences, lives and moves and changes shape even in the moment that we try to observe it. We cannot turn the kaleidoscope to get a better view without changing the pattern we see.

A different image may illustrate more concretely than the kaleidoscope the living nature of faith. Our efforts to hold faith still so that we can control it and possess it securely are like my small daughter's efforts to capture our dog, Rachel. Rachel is basically affectionate and playful.

She is very patient with Sarah. But the moment Sarah tries to capture Rachel, to *make* Rachel be still, or to treat Rachel like a stuffed doll, Rachel asserts herself. She affirms her aliveness and dignity by squirming out of Sarah's grasp and running away to a place where Sarah cannot find her. It is just so with faith. Because it is alive, it resists any suggestion that it can be trapped, controlled, or boxed-in like an inanimate, static object. If we ever did fully and finally succeed in confining it so that it could not live freely, it would die, or at least hide in a corner where we could not find it.

Paradoxically, then, we understand faith best when we recognize that it, like all living things, is ultimately a mystery. Faith is like the kaleidoscope in many ways. But unlike the kaleidoscope, faith is not something we have just temporarily failed to understand. It is something we inevitably fail to understand *fully*. Faith will always be something other than our definitions of it because experience is always something other than our words about it. Faith is mystery. Faith is life.

Summary

1. The experience of faith is kaleidoscopic and can reveal many facets—such as belief, hope, or trust—without changing its essential nature. We have usually failed to understand faith's kaleidoscopic nature.
2. We usually fail to see a common basic nature or experience of faith out of which many related experiences such as belief, trust, hope, commitment, and love arise.
3. We usually fail to realize that experiences of belief, trust, and hope, because they arise out of a common bond, are not entirely separate.
4. We usually speak of the experience of faith very restrictively and are therefore suspicious of those who experience faith in other ways.
5. Faith, in the final analysis, is a mystery. However, the impossibility of gaining a completely adequate knowledge of the nature of faith does not remove our responsibility or desire to search for more adequate insights.

6. Faith is a form of experience. We say this to distinguish it from the content of any particular experience of faith.
7. The experience of faith is an organic part of us and, to the degree to which we are grasped, serves to shape our personal being.
8. We experience faith as ultimate concern. It is an experience of being grasped by the feeling that something or someone matters. Ultimate faith is the experience of being grasped totally by the sense that someone or something matters ultimately.
9. Once an ultimate faith becomes the center of a person's existence, all other elements—all other faith commitments—become measured by and expressed in that ultimate commitment. Ultimate faith unifies the many secondary faiths in our lives.
10. The awareness of a lack of wholeness in our lives—caused partially by a desire for an easy faith—creates within us a desire for a unifying commitment, an ultimate faith.
11. Because the faith experience grows and changes with the rest of our life experience, it is sometimes helpful to think of faith as a process or a journey through which we move, pausing at different stages.
12. The process of growth in faith is often a difficult one. It requires courage to grow into new, deeper commitments and understandings.

Study and Discussion Questions
1. How is the kaleidoscope image a help or a hindrance to your understanding of the nature of faith?
2. If the experience of faith is truly kaleidoscopic in nature, then everyone's variety of faith experiences are, like the kaleidoscope's changing patterns, made of the same basic "stuff." Do you

agree or disagree with this assertion? Why? How might the view expressed here help you to build bridges and form relationships between others who apparently have different faith experiences than you? If this insight is not new to you, what were the circumstances surrounding your initial awareness of it?

3. How are the names you use to describe your different patterns of faith (hope, trust, belief, love) restrictive of broader understandings? How might you begin to view your words describing faith experiences in the future?

4. The author maintains that even though two people may hold different beliefs, they both still experience belief. Similarly, although people have different hopes, they both still experience hope. Thus the common ground upon which understanding and relationships may occur is the general experiencing of belief or hope. How is this insight useful in learning how to better understand those who are different from you?

5. The term *being grasped* has been used to aid understanding of what or who it is that matters. What are your reactions to this term and why? If this term is not especially useful to you as you consider your experiences of faith, what would you offer as an alternative term?

---

6. The testimonies of Jeremiah and Amos are used as illustrations of being grasped ultimately. What other testimonies from the Bible, Book of Mormon, and church history also depict this kind of experience? What are some more contemporary examples of this kind of experience (a well-known figure or personal acquaintance)?

7. Recall an experience in your life which has become of central—ultimate—importance to you. Identify all the elements of this experi-

ence—time, place, others involved, the issue of concern. How has this experience led to a personal commitment on your part? Share your experience with someone else.
8. Why is it tempting and seemingly necessary to think that one or several patterns of faith's kaleidoscope are final or "true"? Would this tendency to finally categorize faith as such be growth-inhibiting and possibly even destructive? What are both the challenges and the problems of holding an open-ended or dynamic view of faith?
9. When have you felt the heat of the "refiner's fire" on your faith journey? How did you respond?
10. Has the "shape" of your faith changed recently? If so, how do you account for the change? How has this been a growing experience for you?
11. Do you agree that faith can never be fully understood? Why? How do you live in the midst of this mystery?
12. What new insights have you received after exposure to the material in this chapter?

_____

_____

_____

Chapter 4
FAITH AND HOPE

Hope: Wishes and Beliefs

Hope grows out of a wish that something will happen. Wishes describe our feelings. They are not claims about what is true or false or about what will or will not happen. Instead they express what we consider to be good or important, about what matters to us. Wishes are not based on evidence, for evidence does not apply to them. Hence wishes are not proved or disproved.

A wish may, however, be wise or foolish. Wishes may also come alive or die. What we wish today we may not wish tomorrow, because we will be different tomorrow. As we change, it is appropriate for our wishes to change also. Wishes and dreams mature as we do. Dreams may expand to include the whole world. We may dream of a world without war or without hunger. Smaller, more childish or foolish dreams may gradually die as wiser, more adult dreams grow to take their place.

It should be clear that wishes, whether wise or foolish, childish or mature, are never true or false. By wishing we do not make claims about what reality is, but only what we would like it to be.

When we believe that something we want to happen may happen, we are hoping. We may believe many things about which we do not care. Or we may wish for many things that we enjoy simply as fantasy. It is only as caring and believing are joined that hope is born.

Hope, Uncertainty, and Courage

As belief involves uncertainty, so does hope. When we know for sure that something will happen, we anticipate rather than hope. Hope is praised so highly that we may be tempted to suggest that it is better not to know some things for sure. But it is a mistake to make a virtue out of ignorance. We live in uncertainty, in hope, because we must. We simply do not know things, especially important things, with absolute certainty. The virtue of hope, therefore, is not in ignorance, but in caring in spite of uncertainty.

This points us beyond desire and belief toward a third dimension of hope: courage. When we are confronted with uncertainties about whether life will be as we hope it will be, we must decide how much we are willing to risk for our hopes. There are two elements of risk. First is simply the risk of caring. Hope sometimes requires courage because of the terrible pain which we must suffer if a great hope is disappointed. Second is the risk of investing our effort and time in a venture which may fail. Investment is always a risk. Thus if our hope is to be more than passive wishing, we must have the courage to risk investing our lives in shaping the future. Because of the uncertainty of life, because of the risk, active hope requires courage. At times we must "dare" to hope.

When combined with courage, hope becomes a powerful force. Without this combination of courage, desire, and belief, we would do nothing. Hope brings many things into the world which would not have occurred otherwise. When we want very badly for something to come true and have the courage to risk for it, a little possibility may encourage us to invest ourselves in making that small chance into a reality. The strength of our desire and courage becomes a part of the evidence which must be considered in deciding whether something is possible or not. Some things only seem impossible because no one cares or hopes enough to work for them.

Hope and Delusion

The danger of hope is that it can become delusion. We can desire something so much that we may convince ourselves it is possible when it really is not. We create a fantasy world in which our dream is just around the corner. In this fantasy world, our hope may be seen as a magical power. We may come to believe that if we just hope strongly enough, our hoping will make the dream come true. But hope is not magic! Awareness of this fact is vital. The Wright brothers worked hard and realistically to fulfill their hope of flying. If they had not faced all the barriers honestly, they would have failed. Imagine the outcome if they had simply jumped off a cliff believing that their hope alone would give them wings.

We must be open to the possibilities latent in the hopes of persons. Yet we must recognize there is no virtue to hope without honestly acknowledging the evidence of reality. The more solidly we can found our hopes on the evidence, the greater our chances of success. Sound hope does not ignore the facts. Rather, it sees possibilities in them which others may not see; and it is willing to invest itself to make those possibilities into actualities.

Hope, Faith, and Realism

Hope becomes a dimension within the life of faith when wishing is transformed into faithful concern. For example, a person might be grasped by a vision of a world without war. The ultimate commitment for such a person would be to work for peace wherever possible. Such a commitment could be largely secular, or it could arise as part of a religious faith such as faith in Jesus Christ as the Prince of Peace. In either case, such a basic commitment and concern would properly be called *faith;* and a basic element of that faith would be the hope that the vision might someday come true. On even the slimmest evidence, a person might well consider this hope worthy of great risk.

So there is a tension which exists in faithful hope. On the one hand, hope must be courageous in its willingness to take great risks for a great cause. Hope must be able to see possibilities where others cannot. Hope must be determined enough to carry through the difficult and painful task of bringing today's dreams into tomorrow's reality. On the other hand, in order to achieve these apparent impossibilities and avoid delusion, hope must be solidly realistic. It must see every barrier and every danger without despair. Hope must know that it is powerful but not magical.

Hope is not a belief about the future held without or against the evidence. Belief without or against the evidence is delusion. This can be expressed clearly in terms of numbers. If the evidence shows that a venture has only a 20 percent chance of success, healthy, intelligent hope does not delude a person into believing that it really has an 80 percent chance. Rather, if we care enough about the venture to take the risk, we decide to work to make that 20 percent possibility happen. There is no delusion, only caring and risking.

When hope is seen as a dimension of faith, therefore, it should not lead us to think of faith as belief without or against the evidence.

Faithful Hope as a Life Commitment

In the largest sense, hope is a way of seeing the world. We may hope that acting with kindness and love will ultimately make the world a better place. We may hope that if enough people are peaceful enough for long enough the world may learn to live without war. At no one point in time can these hopes ever be said to be proved or disproved. They are nevertheless hopes. They are hopes which express a way of viewing and living in the world.

As a way of viewing the world, hope may be transformed into faith. For example, we may have an ultimate concern about and commitment to improving the quality of life for all persons. Such hope expresses what matters to us. As an expression of caring, for example, the belief that our lives can make a difference is not *factually* true or false, even though there is an important sense in which it *is* true or false. This belief must not be deluded or blind. We must recognize every fruitless action for what it is so that we can learn what actions do bear fruit. We must not pretend that mere wishing will change the world by magic apart from the investment of our lives.

In short, as hope becomes an element of a life of faith it must become part of a centered act of commitment which enables the full and healthy expression of emotions, intellect, and will. Faithful hope involves our whole beings in a manner which helps to make us more whole.

Summary

1. Because wishes describe our feelings, not facts,

they may be wise or foolish, childish or immature, but never true or false. Wishes relate to what we care about.
2. When caring and believing are joined—when we believe that something we want to happen may happen—hope is born.
3. Hope as belief involves uncertainty. The virtue of hope consists of caring in spite of uncertainty, not of belief combined with ignorance.
4. Caring in spite of uncertainty involves risk. Risk requires courage. Often we must dare to hope.
5. The strength of our desire and the likelihood of success are factors to be considered when deciding whether or not to take risks.
6. Hope must not be allowed to become delusion. Hope is not a magical force which can turn the truly impossible into the possible.
7. Sound hope does not ignore the evidence; rather, it builds upon a solid foundation of honesty.
8. Hope is integrated into the faith experience when wishing is transformed into faithful concern and commitment.
9. A tension exists within faithful hope between the willingness to take risks and the necessity of being grounded in a realistic appraisal of the evidence.
10. In the largest sense, hope expresses a way of viewing and living in the world. As such, hope may develop into a centered act of commitment and concern. When this happens, hope is transformed into faith.

Study and Discussion Questions
1. Based on the author's discussion, what is the relationship between wishes, hopes, and beliefs?
2. Why is courage an important dimension of hope? What are the risks involved in hoping?
3. Why is it important to ground your hopes in

evidence available to you? In what ways is this insurance against delusion and disappointment?
4. According to the author, where does caring fit into hopes, wishes, and faithful commitment? What is your reaction to this? How has caring previously been an element of your faith commitments? Share an example with someone.
5. When have you used hope as a magical power? What were the circumstances surrounding this occasion?
6. Try to recall an occasion when a hope of yours became a matter of faithful concern—a life commitment? What did you do in trying to realize your hope and fulfill your commitment? What is the nature of your commitment now—fulfilled, alive, or something else?
7. Have you ever wished and hoped for something that never happened and which probably never had much chance of happening? What was it? How might you have prevented any unnecessary disappointment when your hopes did not come true? Describe to a friend how you would re-live that experience with what you have since learned.
8. What new insight have you received after exposure to the material in this chapter?

_____

_____

_____

Chapter 5
FAITH AND TRUST

Trust, like hope, combines elements of caring and belief. In trust, however, these two elements may be either together or apart. Most trust is simply belief based on evidence; but some trust involves commitment and risk. Thus trust may be impersonal or personal. Since both kinds of trust are often referred to as demonstrations of faith, it will be important to examine them.

Trust as Belief

Impersonal trust is something we exercise continually. As with hope, we exercise it because we must. We exercise some trust in our natural, social, economic, and mechanical environments if we are to do anything. We trust the air and water not to poison us. We have some trust that the stranger with whom we do business or who is walking behind us does not intend to do us harm. We trust in the financial system that the money for which we give our labor will be accepted by those from whom we purchase labor and food. We trust that the brakes on our cars will work and the plane in which we ride will not crash.

Because we are constantly confronted with the necessity of trusting various environments, it is impossible for us to check out in advance the evidence relevant to every decision. Every breath we take involves some degree of trust in the environment, but our reason for exercising such trust is not because it is a virtue to be ignorant.

We are able to exercise this trust because there is evidence to support it. We have been breathing all our lives and hence have good evidence on which to draw our next breath. We have driven our cars for years and the brakes have almost always worked. People accept our money and very few have intended to do us harm. The odds and the evidence support the trust.

The odds and the evidence also call for caution. Any person aware of the state of the modern world will chuckle or weep a little over the list of things we must trust. In each case, our trust is being eroded—by our experiences with pollution, crime, inflation, and planned obsolescence. Radios now announce ozone warnings. We hire police and lock our doors. We demand identification when people write checks and we have the brakes on our cars checked periodically. People who fail to take such standard precautions may be referred to as "very trusting"; but they are not thought to be very wise. It is not a kind of trust we applaud. In these ways trust is simply and solely a matter of belief based on and qualified by the evidence.

Trust as the Evidence

The same reliance on evidence is present in most

cases of personal trust. We trust people we know when they have proved trustworthy in most of our encounters with them. If they have consistently proved untrustworthy, we are not likely to trust them.

I knew just such an untrustworthy person once. Regretfully, I worked for him. Not only was he totally irresponsible, but he lied constantly. He would lie about almost anything, whether he had any apparent reason to or not. The result was that I never believed anything he said unless there were other reasons for believing it. If he said he would do something or that something was true, I assumed that he would *not* do it and it was *not* true. His saying it, in my judgment, was actually evidence against its truth.

Every time a person is trustworthy counts as evidence for trusting the next time. Every betrayal of trust counts as evidence against future trust. We usually do not keep count, but we remember, and our memory takes the form of an attitude of trust or mistrust toward the person. We can paraphrase Hebrews 11:1, and say, "Trust is the evidence" which leads us to trust. Our attitude of trust toward someone is the evidence that we have usually found the person worthy of trust. The more strongly our experience has reinforced this attitude, the more we rely on it as evidence.

When the evidence indicates that someone has betrayed a trust, we must weigh the evidence carefully. The person may have been dishonest. But if, over long years, we have found the person always to be honest, that too is evidence which must be weighed against the evidence in the present situation. It is easy to say that trust in such situations is a form of faith as belief without or against the evidence. This reinforces a view of faith which is being argued against. The point here is that trust in such moments is not belief in a person without evidence or even against the bulk of the evidence. The bulk of the evidence lies in the years past. All of that is balanced against the evidence of the present moment.

Trust as belief is based on the evidence of experience. A person who believes contrary to the evidence is not considered virtuous or wise. A parent, for example, who hires a baby-sitter known for child abuse or neglect would not be considered virtuous for exercising such trust. But a person who says "this person has never lied to me" is giving a good reason for believing the person is not lying now.

Trust, Hope, and Courage

There are times, however, when trust, like hope, moves beyond mere belief on the basis of evidence. Sometimes the elements of caring and risking enter into trust. At other times we may decide to trust someone even though the evidence indicates that the person may very well betray the trust. In such times trust is not an act of belief, but an act of courageous caring. Such trust is seen as an investment which we hope will bear fruit.

This aspect of trust should be evident to a parent or to anyone who has had a part in nurturing trustworthiness in another person. How can persons learn to be worthy of trust if they are never given trust? None of us is always honest and trustworthy. We all make mistakes. But we all need to feel that people respect us and trust us despite our errors. The respect and trust of others is essential to our self-respect and self-trust.

Because of this experience, we may decide to invest trust in someone as an act of caring rather than an act of believing. At this point trust takes on the dimensions of both hope and faith. We may say that we have been grasped by the worth of the other person. We are concerned about and committed to this person's development as someone worthy of respect and trust. This is the element of faith in our relationship with such persons.

We also must have reason to believe that our efforts have some possibility of success. In this way our trust expresses both the caring and believing aspects of hope.

Wise Trust

If I have already decided that a person is not presently trustworthy, I must ask another question. Does the evidence suggest that investing my trust will nurture such trustworthiness, or will it only be destructive? If the person simply views me as another person to be used or exploited, investing my trust may do more harm than good. This decision must also be based on whatever evidence is available. Trust should be as realistic and undeluded as hope, even while it moves out in its expression of faith in the worth of its object.

As with hope, there is an element of caring trust which has nothing to do with evidence. Our caring, our being grasped by, our being concerned about and committed to another person, is not a matter of belief in something which may be true or false. Hence our faith in a person is not determined by the evidence of that person's trustworthiness. Our faith is our affirmation that the person matters. When the evidence indicates that the risk may be fruitful in nurturing trust, our faith may express itself by leading us to invest our trust where other evidence indicates that this specific act of trust will be betrayed.

Trust is not belief without or against the bulk of the evidence. Trust may be an act of belief or it may be an act of caring. Insofar as it is an act of belief, wise and responsible trust must be based as far as possible on the available evidence. But in the sense that trust expresses faith—concern and caring—faith itself makes no claims about what is true or false, only about the mattering of the person. This is not a claim deduced from evidence. To be responsible and wise, however, such faith must make investments of trust based on the available evidence about the probable results of such a risk.

Trust as Centered Act

Trust as an act of personal concern shares in the life of hope and faith. It resembles hope in that it involves elements of belief, which must be evaluated by the available evidence and an element of caring. So far as this aspect of caring has the depth of a genuine state of being grasped by and committed to the worth of the person involved, trust becomes part of the life of faith. As such, it will involve a centering of the whole person—emotions, intellect, and will—around a central focus, so that they all work together in healthy mutual support.

Summary

1. Trust may be either impersonal belief based on evidence or personal commitment entailing risk.
2. We constantly exercise impersonal trust in our natural, social, economic, and mechanical environments because we must do so in order to function effectively, not because we deem it virtuous to act out of ignorance. This form of trust is often supported by evidence in the form of past experience.
3. Personal trust is also supported or denied by the evidence of past experience. Each time one proves to be trustworthy we develop a trusting attitude toward that individual. A similar, though opposite, development occurs when one betrays our trust. Our future trusting is qualified on the basis of past experience.
4. Personal trust often moves beyond belief based on evidence into the realm of courageous caring and risk. This is the natural outgrowth of an attempt to nurture trust in others. When we become grasped by the worth of others and committed to their development as persons worthy of

respect and trust, we may invest trust in them and hope that our investment will bear fruit.

5. Certainly personal trust must be grounded on evidence as far as possible. We must ask ourselves whether our investment of trust will nurture the person into trustworthiness or lead to a negative effect on that person and those with whom that person comes into contact.

Study and Discussion Questions

1. What is the relationship between trust and evidence?
2. Why is trust which is not based on evidence not a virtue? In what ways is this form of trust sometimes necessary, while not ideal?
3. What is the relationship between trusting someone without evidence and someone's mattering? Why does this mattering have nothing necessarily to do with what is true or false about that person?
4. How is trust as an act of personal concern a "tendering of the whole person—emotions, intellect, and will"? Why is this important, or unimportant?
5. How is trust in someone not a belief in them over and against the evidence? If there was ever an instance when your trust in someone was betrayed, did the evidence prior to that time warrant your trust in that person? Or did you trust this individual without any evidence as to trustworthiness?
6. How is trust in someone against the evidence an act of "courageous caring"? What is the relationship between your trust in such a person and that person's worthiness in your eyes? Reflect for a moment upon your previous acts of trust and caring and identify an instance that relates to new considerations.
7. Which would mean more to you: someone's trust

in you based on your previous trustworthiness, or based upon your importance (mattering) to such a person? Why? Which kind of trust is more an affirmation of your personal worth as an individual?

8. What new insights have you received while reading or discussing this chapter?

_____

_____

_____

Chapter 6
FAITH AND LOVE

The Unity of Faith and Love

If faith is defined as ultimate concern, then there is a point at which faith and love cross over into each other. Not all forms of faith are like love, and not all forms of love are like faith. However, if we can envision each of them as moving along a line toward ultimate commitment, we may see the two lines of their movement converging until they touch and become one.

Discussions of Christian love are often confusing because it is hard to determine what kind of love we are talking about. *Abstract*, rather impersonal love for "all people," and *concrete*, passionate love for an individual are quite different.

As Christians, we try to love all people. This can be expressed in many appropriate ways and is important when we are asked to help those far away whom we have not met and will perhaps never meet. Such love is also expressed when we act kindly toward strangers we meet, or when we love persons who may be "unlovable." It can, to a large degree, arise out of a conscious decision. "I will give this much money to charity." "I will be kind to Fred no matter how he acts." This kind of love is basically a commitment to the worth of persons and to the value of kindness and caring in human relationships.

Yet a deeply personal love undergirds this more abstract love. When love is experienced as passion, as an overwhelming joy and caring in the presence of another, love is no longer a simple matter of decisions. It is something by which we are grasped in a powerful way, and which involves a commitment to that person as one who matters. To "fall in love" is to be grasped by faith.

Love and Belief

One of the benefits in recognizing the basic unity between faith and love is that we can learn about one by studying the other. In this case, we wish to learn about faith by asking about the relationship of love to belief. The relationship is a complex one which no book is likely to completely capture, but perhaps we can gain some insights.

Belief as Necessary but Not Sufficient

We cannot fall in love with someone about whom we are ignorant or believe nothing. Some knowledge or belief is necessary to the relationship of love. But simply knowing or believing a great deal about a person is not sufficient to make us love that person. Some people about whom I know very much, and about whom I believe even more, I do not like at all.

Love is not a purely intellectual experience. Nor is it a matter of willful decision. The phrase "falling in love" says this very clearly. We do not argue our way into falling in love by weighing facts or logic (even though we may do much arguing during the fall). We do not simply decide to fall in love even though we may struggle with many questions and experience uncertainty which seems to call for us to make a decision. For example, we may come to a point at which we must decide to actively avoid or work for a relationship. Decision is not totally absent. Ultimately, neither belief nor decision is the cause of love. We must finally *discover* that we are or are not in love. To decide that we love someone in this deeply passionate and joyous way is actually to acknowledge something we have learned about ourselves over which we have only partial control. We are either grasped or not grasped.

We cannot say what causes us to fall in love. Both the mind and the will have a place—a vital place—in the experience of love, but there is more. If we are not grasped by love, belief and will cannot simply command us to love in that deeply personal manner.

The Truth of Love

Sometimes the beliefs which have nurtured love are found to be false. We could have been deceived, misled, or the victim of misunderstanding. To this extent we would need to acknowledge that love and true belief are related in some important ways. If basic beliefs about a person are disproved, our love must be reevaluated; or rather, our love will change in some way and we must examine that change and its implications.

Even in this case, it is clear that beliefs about the person are not identical with love. We know a great deal about many people with whom we are not in love. A psychiatrist may come to know many very intimate things about a person that even that person's spouse does not know. But psychiatrists do not automatically fall in love with every patient. If love were identical with belief or knowledge, love would be purely intellectual.

Since belief is obviously not the sole cause of love, change in belief cannot itself destroy love; at least, not every change of belief can do so. One evidence of this is that love can persist and grow while people change. After eleven years of marriage, my wife and I are radically different in many ways than we were when we first fell in love. In this sense, my "beliefs" about the kind of person she is have also had to change. As we come to know people better over many years, we discover both weaknesses and strengths that were previously hidden. But even in a more radical case, where we might discover that a person we love has hidden something important from us, we often find that our love survives that discovery, and may even mature further in the struggle with the new insight.

The distinction between belief and love is made clear in the different meanings the word "true" has when applied to them. Beliefs are true or false as they accurately or inaccurately describe facts. Most beliefs are directly subject to proof or disproof by examination of evidence. But love is not true or false in this way. When we speak of "true love," we mean love which is sincere and loyal. Love can therefore remain true when specific beliefs about a person are proved false. Love can prove false, and even die, while beliefs remain unchanged and true.

When very basic beliefs about a person are proved false, or become false because of changes in the person, love may or may not die. Beliefs are important to love but they are not identical with it.

True Love Is Not Blind

As with hope and trust, there is no virtue in love that is blind. Love that is true is love which seeks to love people as they really are. True love does not hide from facts or evidence. Love which is not honest cannot be true because it reveals a greater concern about self than about the other person. For example, what should we do if we suspect that someone we love very much may be either an alcoholic or suffering from mental illness? If we are more concerned about ourselves than the other person, we may hide from the unpleasant facts, and simply hope the problem will go away so that we do not have to struggle with it. But if we truly love that person, we will have to find out the truth so that we can be of some help. Only by trying, so far as possible, to have accurate beliefs about the person can our love be truly constructive and creative on behalf of that person.

Love that is blind cannot help but stumble and collapse over the obstacles before it. Those who deny the evidence in the name of love have not understood the demands of love. Only love which is intelligent and honest can be of real service. Love that is mature (faithful) embraces the truth.

The Unity of Faith and Love: Further Reflections

Commitment is the key word which describes the unity of faith and love. Love that misses the mark of honest and faithful commitment lapses into various forms of infatuation and desire. Faith which misses the mark usually lapses into mere belief, often sustained by insecurity or pride more than evidence, or into purely emotional enthusiasm.

In true commitment, love and faith merge in the service of that by which we are grasped. Faithful love is not blind, because ignorance can make love dangerous, as in a frightened parent who mistakenly gives the wrong medicine to a sick child. Faithful love makes us willing to risk and hope, and to sacrifice when necessary on behalf of that hope. Faithful love motivates us to know the object of love, even when that knowing is painful, and enables us to rejoice in the truth which makes service and communion possible. Faithful love gives our lives unity by giving us a center and a direction. Our intellect seeks understanding so that our will may be effective in joyous service.

Summary
1. Faith, as ultimate concern, often manifests itself as love.
2. Abstract, rather impersonal love for all people is basically a commitment to the worth of persons and to the value of kindness and caring in human relationships. Such love is often the result of a conscious decision.
3. Concrete, passionate love for an individual is the result of being grasped by that individual as one who matters. We become intimately involved with the life of another. It is not simply a matter of conscious decision.
4. Because of the intimate relationship which exists between faith and love, we may learn about the former by studying what we have experienced with the latter. In this way, we may gain insights such as the following:
    a. While beliefs and decisions are inescapable in a love relationship, they are not identical with that love. We must finally discover or recognize that we are grasped by another person apart from what we believe, know, or desire about that individual.
    b. Since love is not identical with or caused by belief, a change in belief need not necessarily destroy love.
    c. Beliefs are dependent on objective facts for their truth value. The truth of love depends on such qualities as sincerity and loyalty.
    d. True love seeks to serve persons as they really are and, therefore, is firmly based on evidence. If our love is blind it reveals a greater concern for ourselves than for the object of our love.

5. Faith and love unite in commitment to that by which we are grasped.

Study and Discussion Questions
1. What is the relationship—the crossover point—between faith and love?
2. Why is some knowledge or belief about a person necessary to the relationship of love? Why is this not sufficient cause to love someone?
3. What might happen to your love for others when some of your basic beliefs about them prove to be false? How might changing beliefs about someone affect your love for that person? What are the implications of this when you realize that change is a necessity of life and growth?
4. Why is true love not blind? Why is dishonest love not true love? How does dishonest love show more of a concern for self, as opposed to the object of such love?
5. What key word describes the unity of faith and love?
6. Why is a faithful love more willing to take risks than blind love? Why must loving service be grounded in truth? What might happen when it is not?
7. What may be the meaning of the author's comment that "to fall in love is to be grasped by faith"? When has this happened in your life? Describe this event to another person.
8. What new understandings have you acquired from this chapter?

_____

_____

_____

Chapter 7
FAITH AND BELIEF

The first six chapters have included an exploration of the relationship between faith and belief. It has been argued that faith and belief are not identical, but that they are closely related. We cannot be concerned about or committed to something or someone about whom we have no beliefs at all. Nor can we express our commitment effectively unless we have some accurate beliefs about the nature of that to which we are committed. The question, "What ought I to do?" always presupposes some general or specific beliefs about the situation in which we are acting.

My sense of being grasped by Sarah arose with far fewer specific beliefs than my love for my wife or family or friends. Yet I must believe some things about children in general and Sarah in particular if my commitment to her is to be successful in nurturing her as a healthy and loving person. Furthermore, the extent to which those beliefs accurately reflect reality is important. Even though children can survive a great deal of parental foolishness, Sarah will no doubt be influenced greatly by the beliefs my wife and I hold about how children should be raised. Consequently, we want those beliefs to be as intelligent and well-founded as possible. Our faith in her requires intelligent beliefs if it is to be a healthy faith.

Belief and the Distortion of Faith

Regretfully, the relationship between faith and belief has been distorted by the assumption that faith is identical with belief, and that this kind of belief may and should be held without or against evidence. This distortion of the idea of faith has been and continues to be a major problem in most of Western religious tradition, and consequently, for Western society as a whole.

This distorted view of faith can come in very handy when we do not wish to think very carefully about our beliefs, or when we suspect that our beliefs ignore the facts. If new scientific or historical information challenges our beliefs and makes us uncomfortable, we can just say that we must have stronger faith. Should the evidence become clear that our parents are alcoholics or that our children are on drugs, we can assert that we have faith in them, and refuse to cope with the problem. When we are simply reluctant to think things through carefully or to work to really get our ideas and beliefs clear in our own minds, we can escape that task by insisting that we should not challenge our faith by asking such questions.

In short, such a doctrine of faith can very easily become an excuse for intellectual and spiritual laziness, irresponsibility, and anti-intellectualism. When that happens, we are showing that our commitment is really to our own comfort and security, or to our pride in having all the answers. Such distorted faith demonstrates that we do not really care about the object of faith. If I am too lazy or afraid to face mistakes I have made in dealing with my daughter, I show that I care more about my own ego than about her welfare. If we are unwilling to think clearly and carefully about God, or to honestly confront the questions raised by science and history about the nature of scripture, then we are showing that we are more controlled by fear and pride than by our commitment to understand the scriptures and serve God.

Although he could not remember where he found it, my grandfather had a favorite quotation which expressed his frustration with people who have such a view of faith.

Few people realize that most of the things they believe are simply taken for granted—carelessly assumed, without any proof whatsoever. They believe this or that because they have "always heard it"—read it—or been taught it. They simply accept it. It lodges in the mind. It may be totally untrue, but they believe it and often would fight to uphold its supposed factuality. That careless method probably accounts for a large percent of what is in the average mind. Then, secondly, people believe what they want to believe. They refuse to accept what they do not want to believe.

When we look at ourselves in this light, I hope we can chuckle a little and admit how often this is the case. When we think about it for a moment, it seems pretty obvious that we want—and should try to have—good reasons for what we believe. On trivial matters, we do not always have time to worry about getting all the facts. But where a great deal is at stake, we want some really solid evidence and reasons on which to base our beliefs and decisions. That is the kind of responsible and intelligent people we all want to be.

The Origin of the Distortion

If we all really want to be intelligent and responsible, what is the origin of this mistaken notion of faith, and why do we rely on it so often? It has already been suggested that part of the reason is that we sometimes fall victim to our less noble emotions of fear and pride. There are two other reasons.

First, we are constantly required to make decisions and commitments without adequate information. We cannot know everything there is to know, no matter how hard we try. Especially in the most important questions of life, we must decide what is true and right when we do not have all the evidence we need. By itself, however, this might create frustration, but not a distorted doctrine of faith.

Faith as the caring element of hope and trust leads us to take risks. Often it induces us to invest ourselves where the evidence suggests that the odds may be against us. The more the evidence says the odds are against us, the more committed we must be in order to make such investments of trust and hope. In other words, the more the evidence is against us, the more faith we need to have to take the risk.

Given the close relationship between faith and belief, we can easily see how this experience could be transformed (distorted) into the idea that faith is believing something against the evidence, and that the more the evidence is against our beliefs, the more faith we must have to believe them. This is definitely a distortion which should and can be cleared up by careful reflection.

True faith as commitment and caring, as being grasped, always attempts to have beliefs which are as intelligent and as well-supported by the evidence as possible. If we are taking the risk out of hope or trust or love, we want to know everything we can that may help or hinder the success of that risk-taking. If there is only a 10 percent chance that our risk will be successful, we want to know that so we can look for better alternatives or at least assess whether it is really worth the risk. If there is no other alternative that can be employed to achieve a goal, and if we care enough to make the commitment anyway, then it obviously requires a great deal of faith to work against such odds. This problem is usually compounded by the fact that we really do not know what the odds are. We are without all the facts we need in taking the risk.

This is, however, entirely different from holding a belief without evidence to support the belief, or when the evidence shows that the belief is mistaken. That is not faith. It has nothing to do with caring, commitment, or being grasped, unless we are in the grasp of our own fear and pride.

The constant necessity of making decisions and taking risks when the odds are against us or when we lack important information can lead us to confuse the willingness of faith to risk with willingness to believe against the evidence. The willingness to risk on behalf of the purposes and people we care about is so highly regarded as a moral virtue, it is understandable that stubborn adherence to unfounded beliefs can gain some of that same sense of loyal virtue. But the distinction is clear: one is a virtue, the other is not. One requires courage and concern for the object of faith; the other expresses laziness, fear, and pride, or, at best, lack of time to become informed.

Factual Beliefs and Value Beliefs

The second reason for confusion over the meaning of faith is a problem of language. We use the language of "believing" to deal both with facts and values. That is, we sometimes say we believe something when we mean that we think it is true; while at other times we speak of believing in the sense of feeling that something is good or right. The distinction between factual beliefs and value beliefs is sometimes signaled in English by the respective phrases "believing that" and "believing in." The former phrase most often suggests that we are asking about or expressing an opinion regarding facts, for example, "Do you believe that the world is round?" or "I believe that the Dodgers will win." "Believing in" usually deals with values. When we say we believe in something or someone we are probably going beyond mere matters of fact and are expressing values or affections: for example, "I believe *in* telling the truth," or "Do you believe *in* democracy?" Thus the language of belief sometimes expresses roughly the same kind of thing that we mean here by faith, while at other times it does not.

Since faith and belief are so closely associated, this confusion about the language of belief is an important contributor to confusion about the meaning of faith. Regretfully, few people think about or realize the fundamental differences between beliefs about facts and beliefs about values. Consequently, we do not use the distinction between "believing in" and "believing that" consistently, as can be easily illustrated by the question, "Do you believe in God and life after death?" When we make decisions about values—including commitments, love, and faith—we do not limit ourselves to facts. In this sense we are not basing our belief in someone or something entirely on the evidence. This easily leads people to the mistake of defining faith as belief without evidence. This is a serious error, arising from the failure to distinguish between *factual* beliefs and *value* beliefs.

Once again, the example of falling in love may be helpful. Simply holding certain factual beliefs about a person does not cause us to fall in love. Falling in love is a movement of feeling beyond the facts. But that legitimate movement beyond mere evidence does not justify us in using our feelings as evidence for making factual claims. No one will object if, when we fall in love, we speak of the beauty of our beloved, since beauty is highly subjective. But our love for someone does not count as evidence for deciding whether she or he wears false teeth. It is precisely because feelings are not limited to facts that they are not themselves good grounds for deciding factual questions. While we may, in a sense, have faith apart from the evidence, this is not justification for defining faith as belief without evidence, when "belief" means "factual belief."

Conclusion

Although our faith exists in a context of many factual beliefs, and decisions about how best to express faith must be made in light of our beliefs, we must never simply reduce the dynamic, living commitment of faith to mere beliefs about facts. Faith at its best is a form of love. Faith as caring is that element in trust and hope which leads us beyond mere facts to invest ourselves, to take risks on behalf of the person or cause by whose worth we are grasped. The constant necessity to make commitments without sufficient knowledge, and the confusion between judgments about facts and values both tend to confuse the relationship between faith and belief and to generate the mistaken idea that faith is belief without evidence. But if we are to have healthy and effective faith, we must learn to think clearly about the relationship between faith and belief.

Summary

1. Beliefs are necessary, but not sufficient, for a healthy faith.
2. Beliefs must be intelligent and well-grounded in reality if they are to express our faith commitments well.
3. The claim that faith is identical with belief without or against the evidence is a distortion which may be an excuse for spiritual laziness, irresponsibility, or anti-intellectualism. Often this

distortion reflects commitment only to one's own comfort, security, and pride.
4. One reason for the distortion which identifies faith as belief without or against the evidence is that we tend to confuse the willingness of faith to risk with the willingness to believe against the evidence.
5. The language of belief tends to encourage the distortion which identifies faith as belief without or against the evidence. This is because we use the language of belief to deal both with facts (matters of truth and falsity) and values (matters concerned with what is good, right, or worthy of our commitment). Because of this usage, we are hindered in making the distinction between facts and values, beliefs and faith.

Study and Discussion Questions
1. How can the distorted view of faith as belief against the evidence often "come in handy," to use the author's expression? How can this distortion become an excuse, and for what?
2. Given the close relationship between faith and belief, how is it easy to distort faith into believing something against the evidence?
3. Why must true faith always attempt to have beliefs which are intelligent and supported by the evidence? Why is holding a belief without evidence not faith? When are caring, commitment, and "being grasped" present or absent in such a case?
4. The author suggests that there is a distinction between "believing that" and "believing in." The former refers to statements or opinions regarding facts; the latter deals with values (commitments, love). How and why is this distinction helpful or unhelpful in clearing up the primary distortion of faith?
5. Do you agree or disagree with the statement at-

tributed to the author's grandfather? Why? When and how has this situation been true in your experience?
6. Several examples are provided in the chapter regarding the uses (and abuses) of factual and value beliefs. Use the space below to record some of your basic beliefs. After compiling your list, test each belief using the author's distinction between facts and values, to see if your list combines both kinds of statements.

Belief	Fact	Value

Choose one factual statement and state the evidence for your belief. Then choose a value statement and identify the value implied in it (world peace, love, commitment). How may your belief combine both facts and values?

7. What new insights have you received after exposure to the material in this chapter?

Part III

APPLICATIONS TO CHRISTIAN FAITH

Introduction to Part III: FAITH AND BELIEF

In the first chapter of the book it was indicated that faith is a complex experience which cannot be finally captured in words. The complexity of the relationship between faith and belief was especially noted. There is good reason for trying to separate faith and belief in our minds, and this distinction has been clarified in several ways. But this separation does not always work neatly. Faith and belief seem to get bound up with each other in peculiar ways. This is certainly true in regard to questions of religious faith.

In order to indicate something of what is behind the approach used in the following chapters, consider two experiences which are fairly common for people to have or to see in others.

Some people believe in the existence of God or in

the truth of the church or of scripture without also having faith. They say, and really do mean, that they believe God exists, is loving, is powerful, and wise, but they do not seem to be much affected by it. They may go to church regularly and get upset when someone suggests that the Bible is not always correct. But basically, they have not fallen in love with God and do not give their lives in service to the church or other people. They rarely read the books they profess to believe are the Word of God. They believe without faith, without being grasped.

In contrast to these people, others have deep faith without orthodox (traditional) beliefs. Such people may have a profoundly life-directing faith in God, the church, and the scriptures which has persisted through radical changes of belief. They may live out lives with God at the center, making every decision possible with this commitment as the fundamental motivation. They may enjoy a warm and enriching communion with God, the church, and the scriptures; yet people like this may tell us that their beliefs about these things have almost completely changed over the years. For example, they may tell us that where they once believed in God as a supernatural being, they now think of God as a symbol for the sacredness of life and the world, as the ground of personal meaning rather than as a literal person. Where they once thought of the church as exclusive and perfect, they may now view it as one of the many imperfect and culturally conditioned groups of people struggling to live in response to God's love. Or they may say that where they once believed in scripture as the infallible word of God, they now read it as a rich record of human struggles to discover the meaning of life and to call others to higher vision. Their faith has remained deep and powerful (though surely with some changes in direction and emphasis) while basic beliefs have been radically modified or even abandoned.

Although these are perhaps rather extreme examples, most of us know, know of, or feel ourselves to be one of these kinds of people. How are we to understand them or ourselves if we are like them? What do their lives tell us about the nature and relationship of belief and faith with regard to these central religious issues? These are the kinds of questions which implicitly, and at time explicitly, shape the approach of the following chapters.

Chapter 8
FAITH, BELIEF, AND GOD
PART 1

What does it mean to have faith in God? That is the central question to which we now turn our attention. More precisely, in light of the preceding discussion, how are we to understand the relationship between faith in God and beliefs about the existence and nature of God? In this discussion I will avoid being specific about particular beliefs. As indicated previously, this is not a book about God; it is about the nature of faith. Therefore, consideration will focus on the general issue of how and why we may distinguish between faith and belief with regard to God.

This chapter will be concentrated on the mystery of God and on the difference between believing and being grasped.

Being Grasped by God

In the first chapter, the declarations of Amos and Jeremiah were cited regarding the power of God to grasp a life, transform it, and direct it. The scriptures are full of such testimonies. God called Abram and changed his name to Abraham. God called Moses and, despite Moses' pleas of incompetence and his ignorance about the name of God, God transformed Moses into a prophet and liberator. God called Isaiah who, after agonizing over his unworthiness, responded, "Here am I! Send me." God called Saul and changed his name to Paul. God called Cornelius and his family with such power that Peter proclaimed, "If then God gave the same gift to them as he gave to us when we believed in the Lord Jesus Christ, who was I that I could withstand God?" (Acts 11:17 RSV). Many other stories, in and out of the scriptures, declare the power of God to grasp our lives.

The scriptures also declare that this experience of being grasped by an encounter with the power and love of God is open to all persons. A central element in Christian faith is the proclamation that we can be grasped and transformed by God's love.

And hope does not disappoint us, because God's love has been poured into our hearts through the Holy Spirit which has been given to us.—Romans 5:5 RSV

Therefore, if any one is in Christ, he is a new creation; the old has passed away, behold, the new has come.—II Corinthians 5:17 RSV

But concerning love of the brethren you have no need to have any one write to you, for you yourselves have been taught by God to love one another.—I Thessalonians 4:9 RSV

God is love, and he who abides in love abides in God, and God abides in him.... We love, because he first loved us.—I John 4:16, 19 RSV

Faith and Belief: Scriptural Testimonies

Although belief is sometimes identified as a key

element in the scriptural testimonies, this is rarely the emphasis. As will be discussed in the next part, the Bible simply presupposes certain views of God and the world. When the prophets have shared their calling experiences, they have not indicated that they were converted to specific beliefs about God. Rather they were called to commitment to God and to a sense of God's purposes for them. Despite his efforts to escape responsibility for the call, Moses was called to be a liberator by a God whose name he did not even know. Isaiah was called, as were all the prophets, to proclaim repentance to the people. In each case the prophets indicated their sense of being grasped and changed by God's call. They were transformed by a call to a new and radically demanding commitment to a way of life. Paul was called to a new life in Christ. Not one of these people suggests that the call was to theological orthodoxy (traditional beliefs).

The faith described in this book is that sense of being grasped by an ultimate commitment to which the prophets have testified. Surely a person's sense of commitment to God and to God's purposes cannot be isolated from that individual's beliefs. But the relationship between faith and belief, as stated previously, is not one of direct identity. People with very different beliefs may share common commitments, while people with very similar beliefs may have radically different commitments.

The experience of being grasped is not itself one of belief or disbelief. The transformation of a person through new commitment is a fact of immediate experience for that person which requires no additional proof. We experience what we experience: being loved, being called, being judged, being grasped. We experience the fact of our own faith commitments, which call us to live out our lives with certain kinds of attitudes and actions. For example, when we have known the overwhelming love of God being poured into our hearts, we find ourselves loving those about us. This does not mean simply accepting specific beliefs about God or arguments about the worth of persons. We love because we have felt loved.

Beliefs do, however, play a role in shaping our commitments. A conversion experience does not occur in isolation. It arises in a total life context of beliefs, values, cultural attitudes, as well as social and economic structures.

Consider for a moment the story of Abraham and the sacrifice of Isaac. This is surely one of the great paradigms (models) of faith in the Judaic-Christian tradition, and as such informs our discussion about faith and belief. That Abraham could have believed for one moment that God would ask him to sacrifice his son has always seemed incredible. How could one believe such a thing? But Abraham lived in an entirely different time and culture, one in which child sacrifice was not unusual. So Abraham could apparently view such a demand not as a sign of any moral failure on God's part, but as a supreme test of his own faith.

Notice, however, that in the story, which is commonly taken as the archetype of true faith, it is not Abraham's *beliefs* about God which are tested, but Abraham's *commitment* to God. Just how strongly was Abraham grasped by God's call? Totally! Ultimately! Completely! But were Abraham's beliefs about God the same as ours? No!

In the same way that beliefs and values may shape our experience of being grasped, so the experience of being grasped may shape our beliefs and values. Augustine, the fourth-century theologian, defined theology as "faith seeking understanding." When we have been grasped, when we have been transformed, we inevitably reflect on the meaning of that experience. We ask what it was that we encountered and what it is we ought to do. The experience itself may give us only general answers, leaving us to struggle with the details ourselves. We may never be able to decide just what we encountered in such a moment, but we know when we have been grasped and must try to understand.

It is interesting to reflect on Paul's conversion in the context of early Jewish Christianity. Paul was converted to Jesus Christ. In his conversion experience, he acquired some specific beliefs. He came to believe that in his own lifetime Christ would return in glory to initiate the reign of God. In this particular belief, which is central to his preaching, Paul was obviously mistaken. The end did not come. In other specific doctrinal issues, such as the need for circumcision, Paul gradually moved away from the view of the community in which he was first nurtured. The faith commitment shared by Paul and Peter did not give them common beliefs on all issues, not even on basic ones.

Modern Pluralism

This combination of unity and difference has always been visible in varying degrees in religious communities. I have some beliefs quite different from beliefs of some of my friends in the church. And yet, we share many deep commitments in common. I also share basic beliefs with some friends who do not share my commitment to the church. On a broader scale, it is very possible today for a Christian, a Jew, a Moslem, a Buddhist, and even a humanist to share a common, deeply religious commitment to world peace or to work against world hunger. These people may be able to share in committed service to these causes and in some forms of worship which express and reaffirm their common faith commitment. In contrast to this we might recall that there were Christians with very nearly identical religious beliefs on both sides in the two world wars.

The Mystery of That Which Grasps Us

Similar religious faiths can often express themselves in different beliefs because the object of that faith, God, is ultimately beyond our grasp. The God of traditional Christian belief is infinite and eternal while we are finite. We may have some ideas—beliefs—about God, but it is rather foolish of us to be dogmatic about such beliefs. Intelligent and sincere people throughout history have had very different ideas about God. It is amazingly presumptuous of us to claim that the rest of the world is wrong and that only we have the true ideas about God. Even if all people agreed, we should be humble and cautious in claiming any sure knowledge of God.

The Old Testament contains a group of books traditionally referred to as the Wisdom Literature. Two of these books, Ecclesiastes and Job, warn us against making dogmatic claims about our knowledge of either God or the world itself. Qoheleth, the preacher of Ecclesiastes, declares "Reality lies beyond my grasp; and deep, so deep, who can discover it" (Ecclesiastes 7:24 JB).

The book of Job contains another classic statement of our inability to fathom the depths of God's eternal reality. When Job challenged God's right to abuse him, God appeared in a whirlwind. The whirlwind is a marvelous image, not only for God's power, but also for the impossibility of our ever catching hold of God and holding divinity in our hands for examination. God's dynamic character eludes us. To Job, and to us, the voice of God comes from the whirlwind:

Who is this that darkeneth counsel by words without knowledge?
Where wast thou when I laid the foundations of the earth? declare, if thou hast understanding.
Who hath laid the measures thereof, if thou knowest? or who hath stretched the line upon it?
Whereupon are the foundations thereof fastened? or who laid its corner-stone thereof;
When the morning stars sang together, and all the sons of God shouted for joy?—Job 38:2, 4-7 IV

> Where is the way to the dwelling of light,
>> and where is the place of darkness, that you may take it to its territory and that you may discern the paths to its home?—Job 38:19, 20 RSV
>
> Then Job answered the Lord:
> "Behold, I am of small account; what shall I answer thee?
> I lay my hand on my mouth. I have spoken once, and I will not answer; twice, but I will proceed no further."—Job 40:3-5 RSV
>
> Therefore I have uttered what I did not understand, things too wonderful for me, which I did not know.—Job 42:3 RSV

The wisdom of Ecclesiastes and Job is also supported by the experience of Moses before the burning bush. A significant and helpful insight into the meaning of the divine name, Yahweh (I Am), is given by Carter Heyward in a sermon titled "The Enigmatic God."

The people of Israel wanted to know more about this God in whose being they were bound up. So Moses spoke to God and asked God what he, Moses, was to tell the people God's name was. (For the Israelites, there was much in a name; a name was revelation of a person's true character.)

And God responded. God did not give a long list of credentials or a speech about power, authority, and might. God did not "spell things out," but responded simply, "I AM WHO I AM" (or, in other translations, "I AM WHAT I AM," or " I WILL BE WHAT I WILL BE").

God could hardly have given a more enigmatic reply, the sort that would be totally unacceptable to most of us, to admissions committees, teachers, or psychiatrists. We would be likely to hear "I am who I am" (in response to "Who are you?") as outrageous, impudent, defiant, disturbed. Certainly evasive. God *was* evasive. Moses could not pin God down. Approaching God in fear and tremor, seeking clarification, we are met with a riddle. *I am who I am.*

What about God is God saying?

Could it be that God is not being evasive, but clear, straightforward and to the point? And that point is that God *is*, in fact, evasive, elusive, not One to be pinned down, boxed into categories and expectations? God will be what God will be.*

The testimony of the scriptures, therefore, is that

---

*The Witness, April 1978, 5.

to hear the call of God is not necessarily to understand the nature of God.

Mystery and Responsibility

Does the mystery of God mean that we have no responsibility to try to understand God or to have intelligent beliefs? Of course not. When we have really encountered and been grasped by God, we cannot help but reflect on that encounter. We cannot help but *do theology*. The ultimate impossibility of having definitive (final) knowledge of God means that our ideas about God, and about our faith, are bound by the same requirements of intellectual integrity which measure the truth of all ideas. Rules of logic are applicable to all our thoughts, and evidence should be examined and applied wherever possible. We cannot act out our faith commitments if we do not have some beliefs about the nature of that by which we are grasped and the world in which we live. Nor can we serve God effectively if those beliefs lead us into destructive or irrelevant actions.

We are, indeed, obligated to have "faith seeking understanding." It is important to enter into dialogue with others holding different beliefs to test the strength of our views. It is a moral requisite that we strive to meet the common standards of responsible reflection and intellectual integrity. But we must do so always—especially in the audacious attempt to penetrate the mystery of God—with a sense of humility. In the preface to his book *Process and Reality* (which is just such an audacious yet humble effort to catch a vision of the whole of reality), Alfred North Whitehead cautioned,

There remains the final reflection, how shallow, puny, and imperfect are efforts to sound the depths in the nature of things. In philosophical discussion, the merest hint of dogmatic certainty as to finality of statement is an exhibition of folly.

Conclusion

The ultimate mystery of God is one of the key reasons why it is important to distinguish faith from belief. If we think that a perfectly correct set of beliefs about God must precede a valid faith, we will be forever postponing action. If we insist that the only "true" faith is one which shares our beliefs (having confused faith with belief) then we are certain to lose appreciation for the wisdom, values, and faith commitments of other persons. Such judgments prevent us from working with persons whose beliefs differ from ours, even if we share common basic commitments. Instead, we must seek to expand the range of persons whose faith we can appreciate.

Summary
1. The experience of being grasped and thereby transformed by the power and love of God is open to all persons. As is testified to by both scriptural and nonscriptural sources, this is a transformation which deals primarily with commitments rather than beliefs.
2. The transformative experience of being grasped is not itself an experience of belief or disbelief. However, because we live in a context of values, attitudes, and opinions, beliefs do play an important role in shaping and expressing our faith commitments.
3. Just as beliefs shape our faith commitments, our experience of being grasped by the power and love of God works toward formulating itself in terms of our beliefs and values. That is, our beliefs are shaped by what we experience. Once we are grasped, we seek to understand the nature of that experience.
4. Similar beliefs and values may be held by individuals who devote themselves to different faith commitments. Likewise, individuals sharing similar faith commitments may see their commitments expressed in vastly different belief systems.

5. Because we are finite creatures attempting to deal with the infinite, there are many different beliefs about the nature of God. We should always be humble, rather than dogmatic, in our dealing with that which lies beyond our grasp.
6. The impossibility of attaining definitive knowledge of God does not eliminate the responsibility of attempting to better understand and express the nature of that by which we are grasped. Only by exerting our most dedicated and intelligent efforts in this attempt will we be able to serve our commitments to the fullest extent possible. This effort includes entering into dialogue with those who hold beliefs different from ours.

Study and Discussion Questions

1. What is the meaning of the statement, "The experience of being grasped by our encounter with the power of God is open to *all* persons"? How is this consistent with previously held assumptions? Why or why not?
2. What is your reaction to the author's statement, "People with very different beliefs may share common commitments, while people with very similar beliefs may have radically different commitments"? Recall an instance when you shared a similar commitment with someone who held different beliefs from yours. Share this with another person.
3. What are the implications of having common commitments and concerns like world hunger or world peace with those holding different beliefs from you? How do you work with such persons?
4. Identify an experience in which you were grasped by the power of God, that caused you to seek understanding. Despite what may have been your subsequent understanding, was such an experience still powerful and undeniable?

Why or why not?
5. When might you have felt caught up in a "whirlwind" in seeking to fathom the depths of the mystery of God?
6. Do you agree or disagree with the statement by Carter Heyward that God is "evasive, elusive, not one to be pinned down, boxed into categories and expectations"? Why or why not? How may such continuing uncertainty about the true nature of God diminish one's commitment to God? What might Jeremiah or Job say to this?
7. How do you answer the author's question, "Does the mystery of God mean that we have no responsibility to try to understand God, or to have intelligent beliefs?"
8. Why is it important, when striving to penetrate the mystery of God, to do so with a sense of humility? When have you done this? Recall an experience and share it with another person. How do you now view those occasions when you might not have been humble?
9. Why might it be an important operating principle not to insist that you possess the "true" faith, thereby possibly depreciating the wisdom, values, and faith commitments of other persons? Recall historical occasions when this might have been done by the church? When might you have done this? How may you be enriched by another person's faith?
10. What new understandings have you acquired from your study of this chapter?

_____

_____

_____

Chapter 9
FAITH, BELIEF, AND GOD
PART 2

God and Sarah

Reflection on my experience with Sarah may help readers to see that having faith in God is much like having faith in a person. In both cases we are grasped by a sense that someone (or something) matters, so that we become concerned about and committed to another. In both cases, that by which we are grasped is largely a mystery, calling us to a life-long struggle to understand and act with integrity and love. In both cases, there are possibilities of anxiety and joy in the midst of the relationship.

Faith in God means to be ultimately concerned about and committed to God. It means that God becomes the center of one's life in a way which holds all the rest of life together. According to the scriptures, we live and move and have our being in God.

Faith in God means feeling, thinking, and acting with God as the focal point. Mind is not pitted against emotion, nor do emotion and will displace intelligence. All of life is called into unity by faith in God.

Ultimate faith in God does not mean that we have no other concerns or commitments—no other faiths. Rather, it means that *all* of these other concerns and commitments are understood, felt, and acted out in light of that central concern and commitment. Our many secondary faiths find their unity in the one primary faith.

Faith in God does not mean, for example, that our commitments to work, friends, and family become less important. They may in fact become *more* important as arenas in which we experience and live out our ultimate commitment to God. Relationships with people do not, after all, compete with our relationship with God. Faith in God should help to prevent destructive competition between work and family and other activities by setting them in a context which calls us toward greater quality of life. All of life should be a means by which the presence and nature of God are disclosed to us and call us to a life of caring for God's entire creation.

Yet the God who is the object of faith is largely a mystery. It is difficult enough to understand Sarah. Indeed, it is impossible for me ever to fully understand Sarah, to know her real nature, to feel her feelings, and to act properly toward her in every situation. Even when she sits on my lap and tells me how she feels and what she wants, I do not feel what she feels, nor know exactly the best thing to do for her. How much more so, then, is God a mystery to me.

My faith in Sarah both does and does not have a single point of beginning. Partly, it grows out of my concern for human life in general, something we all have. Though my faith in Sarah began to grow stronger while she was still in the womb, there is a powerful moment of encounter from which I can date it. I can say, "In this moment I met Sarah!" But did I come to know Sarah in that moment of encounter? Yes and no. In that moment I knew that I was grasped by her, but I did not know how I would be called upon to express that commitment in the years to come. As we have lived together over the years, my faith in Sarah has deepened and matured. I now know things about her that I did not know before; but in some ways the more I know about her the more mysterious she becomes.

The same is true of faith in God. In part it is something with which we grow up. Even those not raised in a specific religion can hardly avoid the idea of God in our culture or in the sense of wonder in life. But there may come that moment to which we point and say "I encountered God!" Does that encounter give us a full understanding of the nature of God or of the meaning of our faith? Certainly not. The more we come to know God, the more we become aware of our basic ignorance of God as the divine mystery.

Of course, Sarah is a mystery partly because she is constantly changing in ways that God does not. Yet from a human point of view, there may not be much difference. Whether or not God changes, we do. And the relationship between us and God must change as we change. New understandings emerge. New responsibilities arise. New concerns and commitments develop as we journey through life.

My faith in Sarah calls me to a lifelong struggle to understand and respond appropriately toward one who will always be a mystery to me. In the same way, faith in God calls us to a lifelong struggle to understand and respond as best we can in a relationship with a reality which is ultimately beyond our understanding. I may make mistakes in responding to Sarah because, despite my deep love for her, my beliefs about her are not always right. All the love and commitment in the world cannot make me an infallible parent. Nor can all the love and commitment in the world—or the essential mysteriousness of Sarah—relieve me of responsibility for seeking the most intelligent and effective beliefs and actions toward her.

In the same way our faith in God, no matter how deeply it is a part of us, cannot give us infallible knowledge of God. No matter how deeply committed we may be, we can and will continue to fall short in our knowledge of God's nature and will. At the same time, however, neither our faith nor the mystery of God can absolve us of responsibility to understand and act as best we can. On the contrary, it is precisely our faith which calls us to understand as much as possible and to act with the highest integrity possible.

God: Concept and Reality

I have affirmed previously that the ultimacy of Sarah's mattering is grounded at least partly in her ability to participate in and point toward a dimension of sacredness greater than herself. And yet, it is Sarah's own concrete personhood which makes this possible. In what sense, however, can God participate in or point to something beyond God? The problem is obvious. God, by traditional definition, is the truly ultimate reality. Given this assumption we cannot speak of anything beyond God.

Our ideas and beliefs about God, however, are not identical with God. Even in those instances where our beliefs may be essentially correct (and how could we know for sure which those are?), they cannot be adequate given the infinite qualitative difference between our finite minds and the infinity of God. So even where we may insist on the truth of our beliefs, we must acknowledge that they do not and cannot capture God or even adequately picture God. God is beyond us and our concepts of God.

Thus, while there may be nothing beyond God, there is something beyond our concepts of God. *God* is beyond our concepts of God. The concept of God which we hold, which gives form and content to our faith, may be said to participate in and point toward something beyond itself—the reality of God. It is not in exhaustively capturing the fullness of God that our belief is valuable or worthy of faith, but precisely in its ability to point beyond itself and beyond ourselves toward that which is really ultimate, so that we can participate in the divine life.

There is both anxiety and joy in the life of faith in God. The struggle to understand God and how we are called by God to act in the world is a difficult one. We want desperately to have a sense of certainty, to know that we are absolutely right. Yet whenever we think we achieve this, we deny the ultimacy of God and reduce God to the size of our current ideas. Awareness of this means that we sometimes agonize over the shallowness of our understanding, and experience grief over actions which were directed by inadequate knowledge. At other times we will feel that tremendous ecstasy of insight, of sensing that for a moment we have had a larger vision that will give us new food for growth in understanding. We may also feel the grace of God comforting us in our struggle and accepting us as we are, despite our limitations.

Trust in God

Faith in God is often spoken of in terms of trust in God. What does it mean to trust in God? Obviously it means to feel that God is trustworthy. That is, God will not mislead us, nor betray our trust. To proclaim that we trust in God moves trust beyond mere calculation of the odds into *faith:* being grasped by the absolute trustworthiness of God. It means that we are willing to put our lives into God's care. People trust in God because they have encountered something which moves them to trust, which evokes from them a deep response of devotion and of certitude about the trustworthiness of that which they have encountered. For many people, trust in God is like trusting the earth upon which they stand. It is the one certain thing.

But the earth sometimes moves. Is this because the earth is untrustworthy? No. Rather it is because we do not yet understand the earth well enough; we are taken by surprise when it acts according to its nature. The same is true with God. We do not understand God so well that we can always know what God will do. Sometimes the divine Ground shakes, and we are shaken by it.

Without denying the validity of faithful trust in God, there are difficulties which we often fail to recognize. It is not sufficient to say that God is trustworthy, because that is never really the question. All too often in religious arguments we confuse the reliability of our knowledge of God with the reliability or trustworthiness of God's character. As a result we act or speak as if a challenge to our beliefs is a challenge to God.

This error is well illustrated by a young man I encountered while I was a student at Graceland College. At that time a public discussion was going on at the college about a specific religious issue. I published a short article in the student paper, the *Tower*, expressing my point of view. The young man responded with a much longer article in which he quoted a great deal of scripture. We were asked by one of the pastoral groups to come and participate in a discussion of the issues. Before the meeting I sought out the other fellow to ask him how he thought we could best cooperate in clarifying the issues and our respective arguments for the group. Much to my surprise, he responded that he had no intention of attending the meeting. I can still remember his words: "I have already presented my case, or rather the Lord's case, in my article in the *Tower*, and I don't think I should discuss it further."

The young man's words and attitude left me speechless. I had never before encountered anyone who claimed such a total identity between human ideas and God's. In one article in the *Tower* he felt he had exhaustively stated the mind and will of God on the sacrament of Communion. To discuss it further would be to challenge God, to suggest that God had not spoken clearly or adequately. For this young man, trust in God was identical with trusting his knowledge of God.

This encounter has remained vivid in my memory. It has always reminded me of the folly of being too sure of myself on theological issues. It is one thing to trust in God; it is another to trust in my knowledge of God. God may be infallible; but I am not.

This division between trust in God and trust in myself is less clear than it seems. What does it mean to trust in God? After all, the only knowledge I have of God is finally *my* knowledge, not God's. When I turn to the scriptures I am left with *my* understanding of the writer's understanding, not God's (as is demonstrated so vividly by the many different interpretations of the nature and message of scripture). Even if I felt that I had received a direct revelation of God's will, it is still *I* who have encountered and tried to fathom God's will, *not* God (as is again shown by the conflicting revelations people have reported over the centuries). In this sense, it can never be purely God in whom I trust. I must trust in the testimony and understanding of others and in my own experiences and understandings. I never have God's understanding itself. I never know God's nature or will directly. I always have interpretations of God's will, nature, and understanding.

To trust in God is, indeed, to be grasped by a sense of the absolute trustworthiness of God; but it is never without the necessity of interpreting God through our own understanding. We may have misunderstood what God was saying. Our trust in God does not make us infallible. It is like standing on the earth and saying, "This I can count on." The earth is trustworthy and solid. But it is true to its own nature. It is part of the earth's nature to move at times, just as it is part of God's nature to be more than we expect. The discovery of God's presence in persons and events we had previously discounted may take us by surprise just as does the earthquake. This is not because God is untrustworthy, but because we do not always fully apprehend what is truly divine.

Part of the trustworthiness of God and the earth lies precisely in the reliability with which they act according to their natures. For this reason it is important to remember, once again, that faith is not magic. Magic tries to control God, to shape God to our will. Proper faith tries to be open to God so that God can shape us to the divine will. Thus we are mistaken when we say that our faith binds God (or the earth) to act as we expect. If I jump off a cliff, trusting in God or the earth to protect me, I am likely to be disappointed, no matter how total and pure my trust.

Courage and Humility

The conclusion to which this leads us is not that it is foolish to trust in God. Rather, we conclude that it is a mistake to identify the strength of our commitment with the accuracy of our beliefs. Our beliefs give form and content to our faith. Our faith gives life to our beliefs. Faith is not a substitute for responsible, intelligent reflection. Faith is not itself understanding. The experiences which create faith may help us to understand that by which we are grasped. But we must continue to struggle, to live with that reality, and to grow in the maturity and adequacy of our beliefs. As with our commitment to people, so with our commitment to God—our love must not be blind. A healthy faith calls us to seek understanding while acknowledging our creaturely limitations.

The understanding of faith and trust offered here is one which calls for both courage and humility. Trust always involves risk, and risk involves courage. We must be willing to act out our commitments, to give God a chance. We must, as is often said, have the courage of our convictions. We must also have the humility to acknowledge the limitations of our knowledge and convictions. We must not equate our ideas of God with the ultimate reality of God.

The tension between this courage and humility never goes away. It is part of the life of faith. We must not escape from it into a certitude which enables us to hide our limitations from ourselves; rather we must mature in our ability to live with that tension.

Summary
1. Faith in God is a personal faith similar to the faith we have in a loved one.
2. Faith in God is a commitment to that which matters ultimately, the ground and power by which all things exist and in which they have meaning and mattering.
3. Faith in God serves to integrate and unify all of life around that which matters ultimately. This includes a unifying of all secondary faiths. These secondary faiths may be valued as ways by which we express the one primary faith and ways by which that primary faith may be opened up to us.
4. The more we come to know God, the more we become aware of our basic ignorance of God as the divine mystery.
5. The relationship between a person and God—concerns, responsibilities, commitments, and understandings—must change as that person changes.
6. Faith in God calls us to understand as best we can the divine mystery of God even though we

can never attain definitive knowledge. To this end we must responsibly employ intellectual integrity.
7. Beliefs about God are not identical with the nature of God; however, at their best, beliefs will participate in and point toward the reality of God.
8. We must not confuse the accuracy of our beliefs about God with the trustworthiness of God. A challenge to our beliefs is not a challenge to God's nature. Our ideas are not God's. God may be infallible, but we, most certainly, are not.
9. Magic, the attempt to manipulate God, must not be confused with faith, the attempt to conform ourselves to God. God acts according to God's nature, not according to ours.
10. Faith in the trustworthiness of God must include the courage to act out our faith commitment in the presence of risk and the humility to acknowledge our limitations.

Study and Discussion Questions
1. Do your many "secondary faiths find their unity in the one primary faith"—faith in God? Give reasons for your answer. How may your secondary faiths become arenas for living out your ultimate faith in God?
2. Is it true for you that the more you come to know God, the more God remains a mystery? Why or why not? What one experience can you recall which best illustrates this paradox?
3. How significant is your growth and change as a person in reference to your relationship to God, and your understandings of that relationship? If both of these change with you, how might your commitments change?
4. How do you respond to the author's view that people probably make mistakes about their understanding of God? If this is true, need this al-

ter your ultimate commitment to God? Why or why not?
5. What is the value in holding beliefs about God which represent an imperfect understanding of God?
6. How does pretense to certainty of beliefs about God deny God's ultimacy, and thus diminish the ultimacy of faith?
7. In what ways can stability in your commitment to God (and to others) bolster you in times of ignorance and uncertainty? (Reflect on the author's continuing commitment to Sarah as an example.)
8. What experiences with God (evidence) may have caused you to trust in God? How may uncertainty in what God will do in the future endanger this trust?
9. What is your reaction to the statement, "It is one thing to trust in God; it is another to trust in my knowledge of God. God may be infallible; but I am not"? Why is it never purely God in whom you trust, rather always your understanding of God?
10. Why can faith never be used like magic—to control God? What comfort can be taken in this?
11. Is it a mistake to identify strength of commitment with accuracy of belief? If so, how? How can courage and humility help you in times of uncertainty?
12. Has the material covered here provided you with any new insights? If so, what are they?

_____

_____

_____

Chapter 10
FAITH IN THE CHURCH

Examining the experience of being grasped by faith in the church can be one of the most helpful approaches to understanding faith's different dimensions. Some researchers who have studied faith and personal growth have found it helpful to identify four basic ways in which people come to have faith in the church. These are not exhaustive of all possible paths to faith, nor are they necessarily separate. All four should ideally be present in a balanced faith, but it is usual and legitimate to find a single path especially meaningful in one's personal experience of faith. By reviewing these four ways of being grasped, we can see how a diversity in forms of experience can nevertheless express or give rise to essentially common commitments.

Faith Through Caring Nurture

A friend told me about a very successful evangelizer in a rural congregation. Most of the people in the congregation had been brought into the church through the ministry of one elderly farmer. While visiting with people there, my friend was told about the farmer and inquired about his evangelizing methods. No one seemed to be able to tell him just how the man did it. Finally my friend went to meet the man and asked him how he was able to bring these people into the church community. After a little thought the farmer-evangelist replied, "Son, I just love 'em into the church."

Many people are just loved into the church. This is true both of converts and of those raised in the church community. People may have trouble sometimes explaining just *why* they stay members when they find their beliefs changing over a period of time. Finally they say, "I guess I am in the church because people there care about me and have nurtured me."

The experience of being nurtured in relationships of personal, caring love inevitably leads to the sense of being grasped by that community. It becomes part of who we are and of how we experience the worth of our lives and the lives of others. Even if we have beliefs that are different from those of some people around us, we remember the way they have nurtured us, and we discover that we have a deep commitment—a faith commitment—to the people of that community. Faith has arisen through caring nurture.

In the New Testament, the First Letter of John includes a beautiful statement on the importance of this kind of loving nurture in the life of the church as a response to the love of God.

Beloved, let us love one another; for love is of God; and every one that loveth is born of God, and knoweth God.... Beloved, if God so loved us, we ought also to love one another.—I John 4:7, 11 IV

Hereby perceive we the love of Christ, because he laid down his

life for us; and we ought to lay down our lives for the brethren....
My little children, let us not love in word, neither in tongue only;
but in deed and in truth.—I John 3:16, 18 IV

Faith Through Rebirth in Christ

People may also be grasped by the community of the church if it becomes the context in which they have an experience of religious conversion. For Christians, this conversion often takes the form of an experience of personal encounter with, and *rebirth* in, Christ. Many people have found their lives transformed in one or more experiences of great power. For some, previous feelings of anxiety or of bitterness may be changed into feelings of hope and love. For others, a sense of meaninglessness in life may be changed into a sense of direction and purpose. Still other persons feel they have found a personal friend who is now "just a prayer away." For all of these people, there is a joyous experience of rebirth into a new life in Christ.

Some of the most beautiful expressions of this rebirth in the New Testament are found in the letters of Paul. In his letter to the Romans Paul proclaimed, "Hope does not disappoint us, because God's love has been poured into our hearts through the Holy Spirit which has been given to us" (Romans 5:5 RSV). Paul further declared in that letter, "We were buried therefore with him by baptism into death, so that as Christ was raised from the dead by the glory of the Father, we too might walk in newness of life" (Romans 6:4 RSV). For people who find this their basic road to faith, the central words of scripture may well be those of Jesus: "Truly, truly, I say to you, unless one is born anew, he cannot see the kingdom of God" (John 3:3 RSV).

Faith Through Assent to Beliefs

Although an attempt has been made in this book to distinguish between faith and belief, it has also been acknowledged that they are very intimately related to each other. There is no faith without some content. For many people the path to faith is primarily one of assent to beliefs about the church. These people are grasped by the church as the community which helps them to answer their central questions about life and God.

The acceptance of specific beliefs about the church has been a frequent path to faith for people in the Saints' community. Claims about the distinctiveness of the church, its doctrine, and its foundation in continuing revelation have been central to the commitment and participation of many of its members over the years. The strength and quality of faith which has been exhibited by many people who hold these beliefs cannot be doubted. Through these beliefs their lives have achieved a degree of security and integrity which must be admired. For them, it might be said that faith and belief are merged in that they are grasped by the beliefs.

While we must recognize that many such people have very healthy faith, it is necessary in a study such as this to remember the dangers in this approach to faith. When we become committed to beliefs, it is very difficult to be open to new evidence or new ideas. Dogmatism is very difficult to avoid. There is also a tendency to assert that people have a moral obligation to hold specific beliefs. These problems and others must be kept in mind by those who take belief as their path to faith in the church.

Paul's second letter to the Corinthians contains a passage which expresses very clearly the kind of faith by which these people are grasped:

> For the love of Christ controls us, because we are convinced [believe] that one has died for all; therefore all have died. And he died for all, that those who live might live no longer for themselves but for him who for their sake died and was raised.—II Corinthians 5:14, 15 RSV

Faith Through Mission

The fourth path to faith is that in which people are grasped by a sense of the mission of the church. The specific concept of the mission of the church may vary from person to person and church to church. For Quakers or Mennonites, for example, the concern for world peace may be a central element in the sense of calling or mission of the church. For Latter Day Saints there has been a frequent sense of calling to create Zionic communities. For many persons in all Christian churches the primary mission has been seen as one of bringing people into the church, either through rebirth in Christ or through belief in the doctrines of the church.

These different concepts of the mission of the church illustrate the diversity of content which may be present in faith. Undoubtedly many people are grasped by the church as a community called to a great mission. For some, the doctrinal beliefs of the church may be seen as largely irrelevant; for others, they may be central to the church's mission.

People who are grasped by the mission of the church in these different ways may choose different passages of scripture to express their faith. Some who are especially concerned about social issues may emphasize the passage from Isaiah which the author of Luke uses to describe the mission of Jesus.

The Spirit of the Lord is upon me, because he hath anointed me to preach the gospel to the poor, he hath sent me to heal the brokenhearted, to preach deliverance to the captives, and the recovering of sight to the blind; to set at liberty them that are bruised; to preach the acceptable year of the Lord.—Luke 4:18, 19 IV

People with a more doctrinally oriented understanding of the church's mission may stress the great commission concluding the Gospel of Matthew.

Go ye therefore, and teach all nations, baptizing them in the name of the Father, and of the Son, and of the Holy Ghost; teaching them to observe all things whatsoever I have commanded you; and, lo, I am with you always, unto the end of the world. Amen.—Matthew 28:18, 19 IV

Pluralism in Faith in the Church

It has become increasingly obvious that many persons in the church travel different paths to faith. This can create a great deal of tension when decisions must be made about where the energies and resources of the church should be directed. While these tensions will remain with us, we may be able to deal with them more openly if we recognize that all four paths are really paths to faith. People can be very deeply committed to the church despite having very different explanations for that commitment. Our recognition of this can help to relieve suspicions about the sincerity and motivation of those about us with whom we disagree.

It is also important to recognize that these forms of faith are not completely separate from each other. People who believe that salvation comes primarily through belief may be among the most nurturing and socially active members of the church precisely because they are grasped by the belief that Christ called them to do these things. Similarly, persons who see nurture as the main function of the church may come to respect the beliefs of those who have demonstrated this love to them, and may be motivated to reach out to bring that nurturing care to others. The most socially active people may suddenly be confronted in the midst of that work with personal encounters with Christ which can give them new spiritual resources with which to carry out the work. An effort to unify these paths to faith is reflected in the advice to church members that their evangelistic efforts follow a four-step cycle: care (nurture), call (to Christ), convey (beliefs), and challenge (to mission).

In order for the many related forms of faith which exist in the church to become unified and mutually supportive, the people of the church must have mutual respect for each other's faith. The idea that true faith can be found in only one of these paths is destructive. It cuts us off from the resources and people to be found in other paths. This idea will eventually weaken the faith we each have by cutting it off from its proper roots and expressions.

Pluralism is a characteristic of church life. This pluralism in the faith of the church is a wonderful opportunity for creative interaction and not a regrettable problem to be borne with grief. If we all were to emphasize only one path to faith we would be deprived of the valuable resources to be found in the others. As people travel different paths to faith, however, we can achieve both a constructive division of labor and a creative interchange of ideas.

Faith Outside the Church

An interesting fact of life in the United States today is that large numbers of people who share basic Christian beliefs are not members of any Christian church. The Princeton Religion Research Center and the Gallup Organization, Inc., conducted a survey in 1978 which indicated that 41 percent of the United States population were "unchurched," meaning basically that they were not members of any church and did not attend. Surprisingly, however, they discovered that the religious beliefs and attitudes of the unchurched people were quite similar to those of churched people.

Of the unchurched people surveyed, 68 percent indicated that religion was either very important or fairly important in their own lives. Of these same people, 38 percent said that they had made a commitment to Jesus Christ. Large numbers of the unchurched people also exhibited traditional Christian beliefs: 70 percent responded that they believed the Bible to be either the actual or the inspired word of God; 64 percent believed that Jesus was the Son of God; and 68 percent believed in the resurrection of Jesus Christ.

Without offering further examples from this extensive survey, this data can help to indicate the validity of a further observation about the four paths to faith: people may come to faith by one or more of the paths *without* having affiliation with any particular church. They may find a community of caring nurture outside the church. They may encounter Christ in a purely personal experience which is unrelated to any church community. They may believe in God and Christ without feeling a need to join with any church espousing these doctrines. Many people find their sense of mission to the world in organizations other than churches.

Faith is a complex and flexible experience. Two people may have nearly identical experiences with Christ. One understands this experience to be a confirmation of the truth of a particular church while the other sees this as a confirmation of the conviction that church membership is irrelevant to Christian faith. Similar contrasts could be drawn with regard to all four paths to faith.

Differences among these people often arise from their experiences with the church itself. Some people may see churches as impersonal institutions which are ineffective in their mission and dogmatic in their beliefs. They may feel left out or alienated by differences in life-style. They may simply find the church to be unnecessary to their personal faith journey. Yet if the church provides the environment in which the path to faith is traveled, and supports persons in the faith journey, the chances are very high that those persons will find themselves grasped by a deep faith in that sustaining and enriching community.

Conclusion

The four paths to faith in the church help to illustrate the view that faith is not limited to a single content. Faith can take many forms; but underlying all of these paths is the basic experience which we have called being grasped. In every case the path points toward that which is genuinely important for that person and which provides the center of the person's life.

Summary
1. The experience of being grasped by faith in the church commonly arises in one or more of four ways: through caring nurture, rebirth in Christ, assent to beliefs, or participation in mission. Although ideally all four should be present in one's faith life, it is often the case that one form proves more meaningful to an individual than do the other three.
2. Faith through caring nurture is the result of experience within the church community where mutual support, care, and love have led to a sense of being grasped by the community.
3. Faith through rebirth in Christ is the result of experiences within the church community which have led to religious conversion. For Christians this may mean a transformation of individual lives centering around a newfound sense of meaning, hope, and love. Such individuals have been reborn in Christ.
4. Faith through assent to beliefs is the result of experiences in which the church helps to answer central questions of both our secular and sacred concerns. However, the dangers of dogmatism and idolatry must be kept in mind.
5. Faith through mission is the result of experiences in which individuals are grasped by what they perceive to be the mission of the church. The different concepts of the mission of the church illustrate the possibility of diversity of content being compatible with a unity of faith.
6. Persons may be deeply committed to the church through any one of these paths or may combine them. Respect must be maintained for persons who explain their faith in terms of different

paths. This pluralism can be the source of a creative, productive, growing faith.
7. Persons may develop a faith through one or more of these paths and not identify themselves with a specific church community. Whether or not they identify their faith experience with a church community often depends on the quality of experiences they have had with the community.

Study and Discussion Questions

1. To what extent has being loved into the church played a part in your commitment to (faith in) the church?
2. Recall an experience when you felt cared for or nurtured in the church. What were the various elements in the experience?
3. Many persons have had an experience of personal transformation when they felt reborn or converted to Jesus Christ. If this has ever happened to you, how did this experience enhance your faith in the church? How was your experience seen as the beginning of a new life in Christ?
4. In what ways might your faith in the church have been the result of assent to beliefs? How has the acceptance of these beliefs tended to give you a sense of security? How were you grasped by the beliefs? How do you now remain open to changing beliefs?
5. The author cites a sense of mission as a fourth path to faith. When has such a sense played a part in your faith in the church? To what extent?
6. I John 4:7, 11; Romans 6:4; II Nephi 11:43-48; and Luke 4:18, 19 express four different faith views. How are they different? How are they alike? With which do you identify? What other scriptures express the kind of faith you possess?
7. Different people may travel different paths to faith. Though the paths may not completely sepa-

rate, the resulting faiths often are expressed differently. One unifying point is found in common commitment. What forms of pluralism have you found in the church? How were they expressed? How were they different? How were they similar? Why or why not do common commitments help to diffuse the sometimes threatening nature of pluralism?

8. How do you feel about the idea that these four paths to faith may not lead to faith in a church? How can similar faith experiences with Christ lead one person to confirm the truth of a particular church, while leading another to conclude that church membership is irrelevant to Christian faith? How can the church use this insight in a constructive manner? Recall an experience which strengthened your faith in Christ or the church. Share it with another person.

9. Identify any insight you may have received after reading this chapter.

_____

_____

_____

Chapter 11
FAITH IN THE SCRIPTURES

In 1842 Joseph Smith, Jr., published an account of his early religious experiences. In describing his reaction to the competition between ministers of different denominations at revivals, he wrote the following words which are now familiar to Latter Day Saints.

While I was laboring under the extreme difficulties caused by the contests of these parties of religionists, I was one day reading the Epistle of James, first chapter and fifth verse, which reads: "If any of you lack wisdom, let him ask of God, that giveth to all men liberally, and upbraideth not; and it shall be given him." Never did any passage of scripture come with more power to the heart of man than this did at this time to mine. It seemed to enter with great force into every feeling of my heart. I reflected on it again and again, knowing that if any person needed wisdom from God I did.—*Times and Seasons* 3:727, 728

That Joseph was powerfully grasped by this scripture is obvious from even a cursory review of his life.

He believed the promise of this scripture. He believed it to be true. But his belief was hardly one of neutral intellectual assent, as one might believe it true that apples are often red. Joseph was *grasped* by this scripture in a way which shaped his whole life. He had real faith in that passage. It was like a fire in his bones, moving him to action and speech just as had the faith of Jeremiah. His life was lived out in the grasp of this conviction that if he asked he would receive.

Joseph's faith in this passage of scripture had interesting implications for his view of scripture in general. He produced it, changed it (both ancient and modern), and even eliminated it (the Song of Solomon). Although modern biblical scholarship had not yet arisen as a discipline, Joseph was strongly involved in the effort to bring some degree of critical reflection on scripture to the church, as evidenced by his efforts to learn Hebrew. While Joseph obviously assumed the common view of the nature of scripture prevalent on the American frontier of his day, his personal faith in scripture was not common at all. It was a faith which was both powerful and free.

The heritage of Joseph's freedom with scripture is reflected in the decision of the 1970 World Conference of the RLDS church to remove several sections from the "canonical" portion of the Doctrine and Covenants and place them in a historical appendix. In other ways, however, some of us have resisted that freedom, lapsing back into a more literalist view of the words of scripture and becoming shocked and threatened when shown how Joseph so freely made and/or authorized significant changes in portions of the Book of Mormon or the Book of Commandments, even after they were published. On the whole, many of us today seem to resist the freedom demonstrated by Joseph's faith in scripture.

A Literalist View of Scriptures

As in previous chapters, it is appropriate here to consider different beliefs which may give content to a person's faith in scripture.

At one extreme of contemporary thought is scriptural *literalism*, or belief in the verbal inerrancy of scripture. This view is that the scriptures were dictated by God (or the Holy Spirit) to a prophetic writer. The human author essentially acted only as the recorder. Persons who hold this view usually believe that the scriptures are the very words of God, and hence totally infallible.

Scripture would certainly have great potential for grasping those who hold such a belief. It is an awesome thought that one could actually hold in one's hand words dictated (in some manner) by God which reveal the absolute truth about all the important issues of life. Certainly this could provide the content for a very powerful faith.

Oddly enough, however, it is not too difficult to find people who believe the scriptures to be the infallible words of God, and who nevertheless know little about their content. It is the *idea*, the *belief*, the sense of knowledge, certainty, or even power which grasps these people rather than the scriptures themselves. This distinction is an important one for our purposes. A person can have a literalist view of scripture, be grasped by that belief, and yet have no real faith in the scriptures themselves.

Of course, other scriptural literalists would be quick to point out the contradiction inherent in this neglect of the scriptures themselves. A more mature literalist would call us to revel in the words of God, to study them, to love them, and to come to know them as friends. This view would represent a much more genuine faith in the scriptures. Most believers in the infallibility of scripture, however, are grasped so much by the *idea* of infallibility that they limit their ability to know the scriptures as they really are.

In order to know the scriptures fully, to be grasped by the scriptures themselves rather than by an idea about the scriptures, we must be willing to challenge our ideas, to study the scriptures without deciding in advance what kind of writings they are. Although we all bring some presuppositions with us to such work, we can make an effort at openmindedness. We can ask what the evidence both in and out of the scriptures says about them.

More specifically, scriptural literalists often (though not always) insist that certain kinds of questions ought not to be asked about scripture, asserting that it is inappropriate and perhaps sacrilegious to approach the texts with the tools of modern scientific or literary or historical criticism. They may maintain that scriptures are not to be treated like other written texts; they are not to be challenged by comparison with knowledge gained through scientific investigation of the world. Reason and experience may be applied to scripture only within certain predetermined limits. They also may believe that to move outside those narrow limits is to challenge God. Such an approach seems to suggest a lack of faith in the "fullness" of the scriptures.

A Moderate View of Scripture

A more common view of scripture might be called a moderate view. Persons taking this approach to scripture tend to view it as a record of revelations in which persons have expressed, so far as they were able, encounters with the Word of God. That is to say, God communicated in some direct manner with the authors of scripture, but human nature prevented them from interpreting and expressing that revelation infallibly. The cultural, scientific, and historical context in which such persons lived and wrote would have influenced their response to the revelation and also the translation of their experiences into words.

This moderate view usually allows persons to investigate the scriptures with all of the tools available to modern scholarship. It is possible to admit that the ethical, historical, and scientific views expressed by a scriptural author may not be fully accurate. For example, events like the exodus from Egypt may have been made to sound excessively miraculous or supernatural through several generations of oral reporting. Or the world might have been created by God in six or seven eons rather than literal days. Thus, a moderate view of scripture may take many forms with regard to details of interpretation.

A literalist might offer at least three criticisms of the moderate view of scripture. First, the moderate view can take the sense of awe out of the scriptures. There is no longer the sense of wonder at having in our hands the very words of God. Second, the scriptures can no longer be a fully trustworthy guide for life. If they contain mistakes it must be assumed that any passage may be in error. Scripture loses its ability to provide certainty.

These two criticisms lead to a third. Having started on the road of challenging the truth of scripture, where do we stop? Many things written about in the scriptures cannot be verified. More importantly, if the scriptures cannot be trusted to give an accurate account of revelation, how can we be sure they report revelation at all? How are scriptures judged to be different from other writings? As the old adage goes, once you pull a single thread, the whole fabric of your faith comes apart. What is to prevent us from ending up with no faith in the scriptures at all?

Before responding to these criticisms of a moderate view of scripture, let us consider the strengths of the moderate view. They correspond to these three criticisms. First, we can still feel a sense of awe about the scriptural texts. We might feel that these were written by people who had, in some way or another, heard the word of God and translated it as well as they could into human words. These are the testimonies of spiritual and intellectual giants. By reading their words we can share, to some degree, their experience of revelation. Second, because we are prepared to acknowledge their human limitations, we are not threatened by the possibility that a particular scriptural text might contain views which are not fully in tune with God's view. We can recognize an ethical or historical limitation for what it is without feeling betrayed by either God or the author. We are free from fear about what we might learn about the scriptures.

Finally, this moderate view, because it acknowledges the human limitations inherent in scripture, is fully open to any and all forms of critical examination of scripture which will enable the reader to know them better. The moderate view opens the possibility of being grasped by the scriptures themselves, as they really are—with all their interwoven humanity—rather than being grasped only by a preconceived idea about scripture. We are able to have a free and honest faith in scriptures, to be grasped by the scriptures' message, even with their limitations.

Despite these strengths, there is perhaps a valid point contained in the third literalist criticism of the modern view of scripture: having begun to subject scripture to various kinds of criticism and to start admitting certain kinds of limitations, where do we stop? What is to keep scripture from being reduced to the status of any other writings? This question takes us to a third general view of scripture which may be seen as the opposite extreme of literalism. In this view scripture is essentially like all other writings in terms of its limitations and nature. Its power to grasp lies not in any claim to divinely given correctness, but in its own inherent qualities and its place in the life of the religious community. For convenience, this will be referred to as the liberal view.

A Historical View of Scripture

The *historical* view understands scriptures to be the writings of human beings, not of God. The scriptures' writers may indeed have encountered the divine in some way or another, but this gives them no special knowledge which is not available to other persons. They may indeed have had unusually penetrating insights at times (though not always), but so did many other writers whose words lie outside the bounds of scripture. The scriptures' authors were bound by their cultural, historical, and scientific environments even if they occasionally rose above these momentarily to challenge presuppositions about social justice or religious prejudices. In all of these ways, the scriptures are like other great works of literature, history, and religious thought.

According to the historical view, the value of scripture does not lie in any claim it might make about supernatural origins or unique insights about reality. Scripture has three related claims to value—three ways in which it might grasp us. First, the scriptures are indeed great works. Some particular parts might be better than others, but basically they have survived because of their *inherent* quality. Rejecting claims of supernatural or other extraordinary origins need not close our minds to the tremendous power which resides in the texts. The scriptures contain powerful testimonies of human encounters with the Divine, as well as demonstrations of human nature at both its best and worst. There is no reason why we cannot be grasped by these writings and other great writings, also.

Second, the scriptures are scriptures—that is, they are the authoritative writings of the community—because they have a special place in the historical life of the community. Our scriptures tell us who we are and how we got to be who we are. They tell us about our struggles and triumphs. They are almost always the accounts which are the closest to the historical origins of the religious community, as with the New Testament. No other writings can replace the scriptures in this way. The very fact that the community has claimed them as scripture, for whatever reason, means that they have had a unique and powerful impact on the community and its thought.

Finally, the two reasons already given mean that the scriptures will have an unusual power to grasp those within the religious community. Over and over again the scriptures have reached out and grasped persons who have read them. The scriptures have provided comfort and challenge. They have revealed human ignorance as well as given wisdom. They have changed the lives of individuals and molded the life of the community.

The historical point of view actively invites all forms of investigation into the nature and content of the scriptures. Such an open, inquiring approach to the scriptures need not reduce their power to grasp our lives. There have been and currently are millions of Christians in this century who have come to this view of the Bible and have found that it opened the book to them (or them to the book) for the first time. The scriptures suddenly became real and relevant rather than magical and provincial. This very open conception of scripture has enabled many to come to faith in the scriptures.

A Personal Testimony

I first really confronted the nature of scripture during my freshman year at Graceland College. I was taking an English class on the rhetoric of racism. For my term paper I decided to do an exposé of justifications for slavery based on the Bible. I thought this would be an easy task since the Bible, as the book revealing a God of love, obviously could not sanction so unloving an institution as slavery. I found a book written in the early 1800s by a pro-slavery preacher and began to look up the scriptures he cited, expecting to find them misquoted or misused. To my great distress I found no serious errors in his appeal to the Bible. It said what he claimed it said, that God had sanctioned and regulated slavery, and that no one in the Bible ever condemned the institution of slavery.

I was deeply, painfully crushed. I began to carry this news around to my friends, hoping that they would solve my problem for me. But they did not. They first asked me if I had read the scriptures in context. I assured them I had. Then they asked me if I had checked the Inspired Version of the Bible. I had. Third, they told me to pray about it. I said that I had prayed, long and often, but that my prayers had not changed a single word on a single page. The Bible still said what it said. Last of all, they suggested that "That is just the Old Testament; all of that will be eliminated in the New Testament." Had I been willing to abandon the entire Old Testament, they were still wrong. Neither Jesus nor the apostles ever condemned slavery, and Paul at one point admonished converted slaves not to seek release from their slavery. There seemed to be no escape.

The problem, of course, was that I had been expecting the scriptures to be perfect in every way. I had expected them to be immune to the history and culture out of which they arose, and to the moral imperfections of their human authors. I had, in effect, thought of them as having come down from heaven, complete and untarnished by human hands. People who judge the scriptures by such a standard often assert that we must either declare them infallible or condemn them as a pack of lies. But I could do neither. Instead, I decided that if I were really going to be friends with the scriptures I must be willing to be honest with them, and to let *them* teach *me* what kinds of writings they were. To do this I needed to learn to think of them in a new light.

Previously, when I had thought of the scriptures as being perfect, I was shocked and angered to discover that they presented God as sanctioning and regulating slavery, as calling people to slaughter whole cities—"everything that breathes"—in holy wars, and to stone children who talked back to their parents, as in I Samuel 15 and Exodus 21:17. I felt that the scriptures had betrayed me, had misrepresented themselves to me. But that was not the case. It was I who had imposed my beliefs on the scriptures, not the reverse. Once I realized this, my friendship with the scriptures could begin to grow.

The first step was to realize that the scriptures were written by people, by real human beings like myself, who were products of their culture, lifestyles, and inherited beliefs, just as I am. However much they may have heard the divine Word, they heard it with human minds and human weaknesses. Consequently, I should be neither surprised nor shocked that people who lived in a society which practiced slavery should think that God also sanctioned it.

I considered the view that God really had sanctioned slavery in order to speak to these people "at their level." This would enable me to retain the belief that the Bible infallibly related the words and/or ideas God had addressed to the biblical authors. But the price for this was far too high. I could not believe that a loving God could ever sanction the cruelty and inhumanity of slavery. Instead, I began to focus on the many small ways in which the Bible attempts to soften the burden of slavery, and, as I did so, I began to realize an incredible thing. Major authors and figures of the Bible asserted that even slaves have rights! That is a truly incredible thing for members of a slave society to acknowledge.

Gradually I began to rethink my understanding of the whole nature of revelation and scripture. I began with two premises. First, God could never sanction slavery or anything else that was not born of love and respect for human worth. Second, I assumed that the authors of the Bible were real human beings trying to be sensitive to the Divine, but doing so within the limitations of their time and place. Given these assumptions I began to appreciate the interaction of these two ideas. In the Bible I could see reflected a realization that all persons are of worth and that all persons have rights. Given their culture the biblical writers could not hear this clearly. They could not hear the divine Word calling for the destruction of slavery. Yet they did hear it saying that even slaves have rights.

With this insight—that even slaves have rights—the prophets were able to make powerful statements about human liberation and the demands of God for justice, mercy, and kindness. Once I appreciated the tremendous contrast between the kind of thinking which accepts slavery and the kind of thinking which says slaves have rights, I began to celebrate the many ways in which I could see the divine Word of human worth breaking into the minds and hearts even of those who believed God sanctioned slavery. I began to see the revelation of the divine sacredness of human worth as a process extending over the centuries, a process which is still going on today. We are involved in a struggle to hear the divine Word declaring that we can no longer deny full human rights to women. We are still hearing the divine Word proclaiming the worth of persons. It is not a Word which can be captured in words in a book, though words can often express that Word powerfully.

Thus I came to believe that scriptures are not themselves the revelation. They are the record of the ways in which various persons have, in various times and situations, experienced and interpreted part of the age-long process of the revelation of the divine Word. The interpretations of the scriptures' authors are always shaped by their own cultural and personal experiences. They are always distorted to some degree by the sinfulness of the authors. So, also, my understanding of the divine Word and the authors' interpretations of it is influenced by my cultural and personal experiences.

I have become convinced by my experience and reflection that having faith in the scriptures means caring enough to be a friend of them, and that being a friend of them means being honest about them. If I hold them on a pedestal, pretending that they descended from heaven, I can never really get to know them because I can never admit their human weaknesses. If I never admit their weaknesses, I can never really appreciate their strength, courage, and struggle. By recognizing all of this I can best discover the divine Word struggling to break through the human words of the scriptures.

True faith in anything means being concerned enough to discover the truth about it so that we can express our commitments as honestly and effectively as possible. The same is true of faith in scripture. Faith in scripture should not be identified with believing that scriptures are infallible. The willingness to admit the very humanness of scripture is no sign of a lack of faith. Faithfulness with regard to the scriptures means letting them teach us what they really are.

Summary
1. Some persons' faith in scripture is expressed by scriptural literalism, the belief in verbal inerrancy of scripture. They believe that scripture is dictated by God (or the Holy Spirit) to a human author who acts as a recorder. Scripture is, therefore, held to be the very words of God and, as such, totally infallible. Because this presupposition may limit one's ability to know the scriptures as they really are, many are grasped

by this concept of biblical infallibility who have no faith in the actual content of the scriptures. The scriptures are often exempted from historical or literary criticism. Studying the scriptures with intellectual integrity is often deemed sacrilegious.

2. Some persons' faith in scripture is expressed in a moderate view which sees scripture as the product of fallible humans who have attempted to express encounters with the infallible Word of God. The contexts of the authors' lives are taken into consideration and the scriptures are seen as appropriate material for scholarly criticism. Literalists criticize this position as one which weakens the sense of awe of the scriptures, makes the scriptures no longer a trustworthy guide for life, and leads to a total devaluation of the scriptures. The strengths of this position include the ability of those who hold it to share in the experience of revelation felt by the authors, the absence of threat connected with the fallibility of scripture, and, because of its openness to scholarship, the possibility of persons coming to a fuller appreciation of the proper function and place of scripture.

3. Some persons' faith in scripture is expressed in a historical view which sees scripture as essentially like all other writings in terms of limitations and nature. The power of scripture to grasp persons comes not from divine origin but, rather, from the inherent qualities of scripture, and the unique place of scripture in the life of the religious community. The scriptures are seen as basic testimonies of human encounters with the divine and are appropriate material for scholarly study.

4. Scripture is the record of human experience with, and interpretation of, the age-long process of revelation of the divine Word. It is shaped by

its historical and cultural contexts.
5. Having faith in the scriptures means caring enough to be a friend of them. This means being honest with them and honest about them.

Study and Discussion Questions

1. What is your present view of scripture?
2. What are your general impressions of Joseph Smith's apparent view of scripture including his freedom in producing it, changing it, or even eliminating it? How does this agree or disagree with your present views? Why?
3. What are your views on the literalist idea of scriptures, which holds that they are the actual words of God? What is it about the scriptures, that has the power to grasp one—the words themselves or the nature of the words (infallible)? Have you ever felt grasped in a manner similar to the way Joseph Smith was grasped? If so, what can you remember about the experience?
4. How easy or difficult would it be for you to study the scriptures without deciding in advance what kind of writings they were? If you have ever done this, what were the results?
5. Do you believe that certain questions must not be asked about the scriptures? Why or why not? How do you feel about challenging them by comparison with knowledge gained through scientific investigation of the world? If this approach is troublesome to you, what might it say about your true faith in the scriptures?
6. If your view of scripture is more moderate, it will not completely coincide with the literalist view. What are the characteristics of your moderate view as compared to the author's discussion?
7. Do you agree or disagree with the idea that "views expressed by a scriptural author may

not be fully accurate"? Why? Give an example.
8. What is your response to some of the literalist criticisms of the moderate view?
9. In what ways can someone with a moderate view of scriptures still be grasped by the scriptures themselves? If this view coincides with your own to a certain extent, recall an instance when you were grasped by a certain scripture. What characteristics of the experience do you recall?
10. In the moderate view, where does one stop in the critique of scripture?
11. What are your reactions to the historical view of scripture? Does this view more closely resemble yours than either of the other two views? Why or why not? If not, have you ever known someone with this view? How did you deal with that person's commitment or beliefs?
12. How might scriptures grasp those who hold a historical view of them? If this is your view, how are you grasped by them?
13. Do you have a testimony similar to the author's in which he related his struggle with the nature of scripture? If so, what is it?
14. How can the view that the scriptures were written by people "just like me" serve to reinforce their value to you?
15. The author stated two premises in reunderstanding the whole nature of revelation and scripture (first, that God could never sanction anything not born of love and respect for human worth and, second, that the understanding of biblical authors was limited to their time and place). In what ways do you agree or disagree with these two premises? Why?
16. How does the author's view of faith (being grasped, committed to, seeking understanding) apply to the nature of scripture?

17. What have you learned as a result of studying the material in this chapter?

_____

_____

_____

Chapter 12
FAITH IN CHRIST

Faith in Christ lies at the heart of Christian faith. For that very reason, it is astounding to witness the amazing variety of forms that faith can take. Beliefs about Christ and feelings about those beliefs differ widely. This diversity is threatening to some Christians. Consequently, there is a tendency to ignore or dismiss forms of faith in Christ which are not like ours. We may even insist that a person who does not share our beliefs and our attitudes about Christ does not have real faith. Perhaps this view might change if we look briefly at the meaning of faith in Christ through some of the forms that faith can take.

Three sample approaches to faith in Christ may be viewed through the testimonies of three imaginary but representative Christians: Drew, Carol, and Joan.

Drew: Jesus Christ is the center of my life. He is my friend, my Lord, and my Savior. Jesus died for me. Jesus is alive today and works in my life.

I believe that Christ is the Son of God. He was with God from the beginning and, indeed, is God. Jesus was born of the virgin Mary through the power of the Holy Spirit. He lived without sin and showed us how we should live, too. Finally, he died on the cross to atone for our sins and free us from the power of hell. After three days Jesus was resurrected in the flesh. Jesus still lives today and hears our prayers.

Jesus is my friend. I talk to him all the time. Some people have even seen Jesus. Someday I would like to see Jesus, too, and walk and talk with him face-to-face. I believe I will someday. Until then, I am happy just knowing that Jesus is near me and hears my prayers. He helps me out and watches over me.

The Jesus I know in my life today is the same Jesus who walked and talked so long ago in Palestine. Jesus is truly God but he is also truly human. How that can be true is a mystery, but I believe it is true. Reading the scriptures helps me to know him and to learn about him. The scriptures teach me that he died to show God's love for me and to make it possible for me to be saved. To be saved, you only have to believe in Jesus and take him into your life. Then someday you can walk and talk with him too.

Carol: Faith in Christ is at the center of my life. Although I don't always understand some of the things I believe about Christ, I think they are basically true. The scriptures, especially the New Testament, teach us about Christ. They say that he was the Son of God. That he was actually God incarnate is testified to by Paul and other biblical writers. That part is hard for me to understand—what it means for Christ to be God incarnate, in the flesh. But I believe it to be true.

The New Testament tells us a lot about Jesus, but I realize that the Gospels aren't really historical accounts in the sense we mean today. The Gospels are more like testimonies about Jesus, so the authors were more concerned about declaring their faith than in giving accurate, objective accounts of the life of Jesus. That is especially true with things like the resurrection. I believe in the resurrection, but I'm not sure just exactly what happened. I don't really think Jesus is walking around somewhere in a body bearing marks of the crucifixion. That doesn't make sense to me. Yet I do believe that Christ is alive in some way, and is with God. I pray to God in Christ's name, because Christ showed me how much God loves me. As Paul says, "God was in Christ reconciling the world to himself" (II Corinthians 5:19 RSV).

There is a lot about Christ that I don't understand. But I do believe that Jesus was in some way divine, the Son of God, and that by living and dying, Jesus showed God's love for me. That is what I mean when I say that faith in Christ is the center of my life. Knowing that God loves me that much makes everything different.

Joan: The biblical picture of Christ is the central symbol of my life. It captures me with a power no other symbol has. It helps me to understand and cope with life, and gives me a way to think about and relate to God.

I know enough about the Bible to realize that the Gospels are testimonies of faith, and not historical accounts. They probably report a lot of accurate information about the life of Jesus, but also include stories that are more like legends or sermon illustrations. That doesn't matter to me very much, because it is precisely the faith-pictures of Christ painted by the various writers which grasp me.

Obviously something exciting and wonderful happened to the disciples who followed Jesus. He changed their lives. Through him they came to know God in a different way. They were convinced that Jesus died because he loved them and because God loved them. Soon after his death, the spirit they felt when they were with Jesus revived, and they felt as if he were alive again.

It really isn't very important to me to know the details about the life of Jesus. I don't believe that he was God, that he walked on water, or that he was literally resurrected from the dead. Yet when I read the testimonies of those who knew him, and reflect on the image of Jesus as the Christ which they present, I am really captivated by the power of that symbol of love and sacrifice.

The symbol of the Christ helps me to make sense out of God. God is so big and mysterious. Somehow I think the disciples were right in saying that Jesus taught us about God. Surely God is loving and caring and chastising and suffering and calling us to new life. Faith in the symbol of Christ is what makes sense out of life for me. It convinces me that life has possibilities for love that real people can achieve. That gives me great joy and hope.

Drew, Carol, and Joan all have very strong faith in Christ; but their beliefs about Jesus differ greatly. Drew has very literal beliefs about Jesus as the Son of God, who was resurrected and is alive today. Carol shares these beliefs in a more moderate and cautious way. She believes that Jesus was God incarnate, but she is not tied to any particular under-

standing of that belief. The same is true of her belief in the resurrection. She generally accepts the biblical accounts of Jesus, but is aware that these accounts are not always historically reliable. Still, she accepts a moderate form of the traditional Christian creeds. Joan does not share any of the traditional beliefs in a literal way. For her, it is the symbol of Christ which is important. The picture of Christ presented in the scriptures captures her imagination and faith apart from any questions about the accuracy of the pictures. The image of Christ helps her make sense out of her own life and her relationship to God.

The view of faith taken in this book enables us to acknowledge that all three of these people may have genuine commitments worthy of our respect, even though their beliefs differ radically. We cannot identify faith with belief so as to insist that only those who share our beliefs about Christ can have true faith in Christ. This open view of faith also forces us to recognize that they cannot all be equally justified in their beliefs. Faith is not a license to believe whatever we wish about Christ. It is rather a commitment which drives us to seek the best available understanding of Christ in terms of what we can honestly know about history, scripture, the nature of revelatory experience, and the nature of the world in general.

To say what it really means to have faith in Christ is tremendously difficult since it is so hard to say what "Christ" really means. Is the meaning of Christ determined primarily by historical inquiry, personal religious experience, life in the church community, or some combination of these and other sources? Do we mean by Christ simply to speak of Jesus, a man who lived and died long ago but whom we now remember as the founder of our tradition? Do we mean a resurrected person existing in a supernatural body somewhere in space who might visit us if we live very "spiritual" lives? While we cannot digress so far from our study of the nature of faith as to spend a long time on any of these questions, we cannot adequately understand the nature of faith in Christ without some brief discussion of them.

Let us begin with the question of our knowledge of the historical Jesus as presented in the New Testament, for this is surely where all people discussing Christ must find their basic common ground. We have already seen that faith in scripture cannot mean ignoring the human authorship of scripture. In this case we must recognize that modern biblical scholarship has made it clear that the Gospels are not reliable historical documents. They are themselves testimonies of faith rather than objective accounts. The stories they tell, the ways in which they tell them, and the order in which the stories are arranged all arise out of the concerns of the authors' communities as much as or more than out of historical fact. Consequently, while we can make some educated guesses about the life and teachings of Jesus and say a few things with confidence, we cannot be certain about what Jesus said or did. The New Testament, for example, leaves us with very good reason to think that Jesus expected the world to end within the lifetime of his hearers. Paul unquestionably believed this. This is certainly troubling to people like Drew; but merely asserting "on faith" that Jesus could not have been mistaken on such a topic is not a valid appeal to faith.

Similarly, we must recognize that the people who wrote the New Testament lived in a radically different thought-world than we do. They thought the world was flat with a dome over it, that heaven was on top of the dome, that hell was a place inside the earth, and that clouds could act as celestial elevators. Having no alternative explanations, they thought that God directly caused the sparrow to fly, the sun to rise, and the rain to fall through literal windows in the dome of heaven. Their understanding of Jesus arose within this view of the world and reflects it. Thus we cannot simply accept their pictures of his miraculous activities without acknowledging this vast difference between their thought-world and ours. Faith demands that we not automatically accept inherited beliefs about Jesus without careful reflection on the ways in which our received accounts of him were shaped by such an understanding of the world.

Now some brief consideration will be given to the question of personal religious experience as an approach to the meaning of "Christ." How do we understand the experience of those who testify of having met Jesus as a personal being, those represented by our fictional character Drew? His views are rooted in powerful personal experiences. There can be no doubt that many Christians today have experiences which they feel they can only interpret as personal encounters with the resurrected Jesus. That such experiences often have great power to shape the lives of these people is equally obvious; and we can celebrate when such lives are made more whole and loving.

Acknowledgment of the presence and power of such experiences does not, however, automatically compel us to accept these persons' interpretations of the cause of their experiences. I can speak from my own experience in saying that our interpretations of such experiences can change greatly. As a youth I also had religious experiences in which I felt love pour into my life. Those experiences influenced my life then and have continued to be central elements in my thinking today. Yet my understanding of what caused those experiences, and what they say about the nature of God and Christ, has changed dramatically. As I have lived longer and made a profession of exploring such issues, I have come to see that these experiences are not necessarily reliable guides to the nature of reality, however much they may change our personal feelings and perspectives. I have especially come to recognize that we cannot appeal to such experiences as *evidence* for deciding historical or scientific questions, such as those about the historical Jesus or the origin of the world. In short, these revelatory experiences may disclose meanings and values to us, but it is questionable whether they can ever disclose factual information.

I recall being angered by a pamphlet which made obviously false statements about the Saints' church. I went to the people who distributed the pamphlet with evidence in hand which unquestionably refuted the charges, but they refused even to look at my evidence. Their answer dramatically demonstrated the dangers of abusing both faith and religious experience. "We just give the pamphlet out," they said. "People can take it home and pray about it. If they get a burning in their bosom they will know it is true, if not they will know it is false." Their preference for such a subjective method over the examination of hard, objective evidence convinced me that they did not care very much for the truth.

Further difficulties must be faced by those who, whether on historical or personal grounds, claim that we should understand "Christ" to refer to a resurrected Jesus who lives today in some form of spiritual body. How can we make sense of the fact that this Christ absents himself from a world so desperately in need of him? How could a being so filled with love retreat to some "heavenly" space rather than be constantly working in direct ways to guide those who seek to discover the truth and to help those in need? It will not do to say that he is working invisibly. For the claim under discussion is that Christ has come to a few Christians as an individual person to minister to their needs. Why only to them? Again, the answer that Jesus will come to any who will receive him will not do, for it can only mean that other people are somehow not as righteous, not as spiritual, not as sincere in their prayer as those who have such experiences.

Clearly those who claim that Christ has come to them in response to their righteousness must see that they risk appearing to have the greatest degree of spiritual arrogance—and it is an appearance which can all too easily become a reality. That such persons do not intend to be arrogant, that they are usually very kind and loving people who sincerely believe that the ministry of Christ is available to all, does not solve the problem raised by the broader perspective. Though their experiences may be personally powerful, they do not seem to account for the larger world in which we live. A faith which is searching for the truth, rather than for mere personal comfort, must give equally serious consideration both to the power of these experiences and to the problems which they raise.

Historical and theological questions like those just discussed have led an increasing number of devout Christians in this century to search for alternative understandings of what it means to have faith in Christ. Millions of these people have found it religiously satisfying and intellectually responsible to speak of "Christ" as a symbol. This symbol is rooted in the actual life of the historical Jesus and in the faith testimonies of the New Testament writers. Confronted with the fact that we cannot have accurate knowledge of Jesus, and that what we do know is often problematic with regard to traditional views of his divinity, many Christians have been forced to read the New Testament with new eyes. They have found a solid foundation in the Christ of faith whom they encounter there.

It is crucial to realize that the Christ we meet in the New Testament texts is the Christ of the New Testament authors' faith. These accounts are their "faith-pictures" of Christ, transmitted and responded to by Christian communities over the centuries, which provide our common ground today. The authors did not give us cold, objective, noncommittal accounts of Jesus. They gave us instead testimonies of what had happened in their lives, expressed in sermons, teachings, and faith stories about Jesus as their Christ. It is this total faith-picture of Christ which is so influential in Joan's life. By studying the faith of the New Testament writers she is enabled to make more sense out of her own life. She has adopted their central symbol as her own.

Here again, I can bear my own testimony. I cannot claim to know much about the historical Jesus. I am too well aware of the problems involved in such a claim. Yet I am powerfully shaped and grasped by the faith-picture—by the symbol—of Christ which I encounter in reading the New Testament. Like the Apostle Paul, I find that I must "preach Christ crucified,...the power of God, and the wisdom of God" (I Corinthians 1:23, 24 IV).

Let it again be said that the view of faith affirmed in this book does not automatically lead us to any particular set of beliefs about Christ. Rather, reasons have been shown why faith as commitment to the truth about "Christ" must not blindly accept inherited beliefs in which that faith has been expressed. Faith must never close us off to honest examination of the evidence which may challenge our beliefs. The "liberal" must, of course, be as open to responsible "conservative" positions as the conservative must be to more liberal views. If any of us are afraid to face such challenges, we show that our real commitment is not to the truth at all, but to our own sense of security and pride in the "truth" of our particular beliefs.

These differences of belief are important. They may mean that the faiths of those who hold them are very different. Yet in some ways our faiths still have a common focus. We all still go to the scriptures to meet Christ. The scriptures help us to reflect on the meaning of who Jesus was and what he means to us. Although we might disagree about the nature and meaning of those scriptures and of the Christ about whom they testify, there is still that common foundation to which we turn.

Regardless of how our beliefs may differ, our faith in Christ should express itself in discipleship. Certainly different beliefs will influence our understanding of discipleship. When faith is understood as commitment, however, we cannot honestly claim to be faithful to Christ while ignoring the work to which the scriptural Christ calls us. Because all who claim faith in Christ must go to the scriptures to meet that Christ, we will all confront the same demands for love and service. Who can read the story of the judgment in Matthew 25, or Jesus' declaration that he came in the spirit of liberation in Luke 4:18 without acknowledging that Christ calls us to feed the hungry, work for peace, and seek liberation of the oppressed? Thus our differences of belief need not ultimately prevent us from sharing in a common cause, testifying that it is faith in Christ which has stirred us to action and rejoicing together in the hope and joy we share through that faith.

Differences and tensions between those of us represented by Drew, Carol, and Joan will persist. Yet each of us will be called back to concern and love for others by the same picture of Christ as the one who lived for others and died for all. We may challenge each other's beliefs, but we can be held together in common cause by the faith, whether literal or symbolic, that whatsoever we do to the least of these, we do to Christ.

Summary

1. Faith in Christ lies at the heart of Christian faith. This faith is expressed in a wide variety of beliefs and attitudes about Christ. The resulting di-

versity is seen as a threat by some Christians.
2. Different persons—for example, Drew, Carol, and Joan—may experience genuine faith commitments even though they hold radically different beliefs. This is because faith is not identical with the beliefs by which it is expressed.
3. Faith drives us to seek better understandings of Christ in order to better express that faith.
4. It is difficult to understand the phrase "faith in Christ" because it is difficult to understand the concept "Christ."
5. All discussions of Christ find their common ground in the New Testament which is a collection of testimonies of faith and not an objective account of history. Therefore, we cannot be completely certain about what Jesus said or did. The New Testament authors were conditioned by a world view much different than ours. We must realize that this different world view is reflected in their understanding of Jesus.
6. Acknowledgment of the presence and power of experiences which some interpret as personal encounters with the resurrected Jesus does not automatically compel us to accept such interpretations of the cause of these experiences. These revelatory experiences may disclose meanings and values to us, but it is questionable whether they can ever disclose factual information. A faith which searches for the truth must give equally serious consideration both to the power of these experiences and to the problems which they raise.
7. Because of the problems involved in gaining historical knowledge of Jesus, many people have found it religiously satisfying and intellectually responsible to speak of Christ as a symbol. This symbol is rooted in the powerful faith-pictures of the New Testament authors.
8. Faith must never prohibit honest examination of

evidence which may challenge our inherited beliefs about Christ. To do so would be to show that our commitment is not to Christ, but rather to our own sense of security and pride.
9. However much our beliefs may vary, our faith in Christ should express itself in the commitment of discipleship to which we are all called by the scriptural Christ. This is what binds together the faith of all Christians.

Study and Discussion Questions

1. Have you ever been tempted to ignore or dismiss forms of faith in Christ which are not like yours? Why? When have you insisted that someone with different beliefs or attitudes about Christ did not have real faith? After your exposure to the material in the book, particularly this chapter, how do you feel about this subject?
2. Which view of faith in Christ most closely parallels your own view: Drew's, Carol's, or Joan's? What elements of that view would you eliminate? What might you add to make it even closer to your view?
3. Would you agree that each view represents that person's faith in Christ, though the beliefs vary widely? Why or why not?
4. Even though your personal view of faith in Christ may differ from those of others, what enables you to respect the commitments of others based on those differing views or faiths?
5. What meaning of Christ, for you, serves as the foundation of your faith in Christ? Has this always been the case, or has this meaning changed? How do you account for either the unchanging or the changing nature of your view?
6. How may the unreliability of the gospels as historical documents prove to be an impediment to your view of Jesus?
7. How can the meaning of Jesus transcend his-

torical accounts of him in such a way as to nevertheless instill faith in him?
8. The author suggests that revelatory experiences and encounters may very powerfully disclose meanings and values, while not disclosing any factual information. Do you agree or disagree? Why? Which, for you, is most important: experiencing a sense of power—being grasped, meanings and values—or factual information? Why?
9. What is your response to the questions posed by the author on page 150?
10. What are your reactions to the author's statements regarding spiritual arrogance? Have you ever been guilty of this? If so, what were the circumstances surrounding the occasion?
11. Is Christ a symbol for you? If so, of what?
12. In what ways can the faith-pictures of Christ in the New Testament be valuable, even though they are not "cold, objective, noncommittal accounts of Jesus"?
13. Do you agree that faith as commitment can more easily express itself in discipleship than can faith as belief? Why or why not?
14. Describe any new understandings you may have received based on this chapter.

_____

_____

_____

Part IV

FAITH AND BELIEF: A HISTORY OF THE WORDS

Chapter 13
FAITH AND BELIEF IN THE ENGLISH LANGUAGE AND THE BIBLE

Language changes. The assertion contained in this section—based on the work of Wilfred Cantwell Smith, Harvard historian of religion—is that the meanings of the words *faith* and *belief* have undergone a radical transformation which has caused readers of the Bible in English to significantly misunderstand the Bible with regard to the nature of faith. Because the Bible is so extensive and complex, it would be foolish to say that it contains only one view of the nature of faith. Counter examples to any such claim will be found. Nevertheless a valid generalization can be made about the biblical concepts of faith and belief which will force many of us—it has certainly forced me—to learn to rethink the way we read the Bible.

Stated briefly, the claim is that the word *believe* is

most commonly used in the Bible to mean something very different from what it means in modern English. We normally use believe to mean being of the opinion that a statement is factually correct. A person who does not believe a true statement is said to be in error, and we assume that the solution to that problem is to provide that person with the correct information. It is common for us to say that we believe things when we do not have enough evidence to assert with confidence that we know them. Thus we may know that the world is not flat; but we believe it will probably rain today. Belief is something displaced by knowledge. Further, belief is not usually related to any personal loyalty or commitments. Belief in the devil is of the same logical type as belief in God. That is, believing does not automatically involve worshiping or obeying. Believing in the devil indicates nothing about whether a person worships God or Satan.

In stark contrast, the Bible most commonly uses the word believe to mean "belove" or "obey" or something related to these. Belief is primarily a value term. It is concerned with commitments and love, not with opinions about facts. The biblical writers did not use the word belief to refer to a secondary form of knowledge. Rather, belief presupposes knowledge in the biblical sense of knowledge as intimate personal acquaintance. Thus the opposite of believing the truth is not error but loving the lie. One cannot believe in both God and Baal, because to believe is to give wholehearted loyalty.

In modern English, believing usually means holding an opinion about statements and facts. In the Bible believing usually means loving and obeying, especially God or persons. Since in both the Bible and in modern English the word faith is closely tied to the word believe, when we misunderstand the biblical meaning of the latter, we almost inevitably misunderstand the former.

History of the English Word "Believe"

The *American Heritage Dictionary* contains an appendix listing the Indo-European roots of English words. The entry under *believe* in that dictionary refers one to the root word "leubh-." In slightly abbreviated form, and with italics added, the entry in the appendix reads as follows:

Leubh-. **To care, desire; love.** I.... In Old English *lēof*, dear, beloved: LEMAN, LIEF, LIVELONG. II.... 1. German **laubo* in: a. Old English *lēaf*, permission (❮ "pleasure, approval"):... in Old English *gelēafa, belēafa* (bi- Be-), *belief, faith;* BELIEF. 2. Germanic **galaubjan*...**'to hold dear,' esteem, trust**, in Old English *gelēfan, belēfan*...to believe, trust: BELIEVE. III.... **lubh-* 1. Suffixed from **lubh-ā-* in Germanic *lubo*, in Old English, *lufu, love:* LOVE. 3. Suffixed (stative) from **lubh-ē-* in Latin *libēre*, **to be dear,** be pleasing: QUODLIBET. 3. Latin *libīdō*, pleasure, desire: LIBIDO.[1] (Bold type emphasis added.)

Without concern for technicalities, it is easy to see from a glance at the emphasized portions that Wilfred Cantwell Smith is entirely correct in his assertion that

The word "believe," then, began its career in early modern English meaning "to belove," "to regard as lief," to hold dear, to cherish. The object (if any) of the verb was for many centuries primarily, and often only, a person, as with the cognate term, "love." All other meanings are derived. To believe a person, or to believe "in," or "on," or for a time "to" or "of," a person, was to orient oneself towards him or her with a particular attitude or relationship, of esteem and affection, also trust—and more earnestly, of self-giving endearment.[2]

Smith offers two striking illustrations. First, he cites a thirteenth-century poem in which a knight is urged to believe the oath he had sworn.[3] The knight had two means of denying his oath. He could either lie by pretending that he had never sworn such an oath, or he could admit to the oath but renounce it. In either case he would have to make a liar of himself, refusing to be honorable, trustworthy, or loyal to his own integrity. In the demand that he believe his own oath he is obviously not asked to be of the opinion that he made it. Instead, he is asked first to acknowledge what he and his hearers know to be true—that he swore the oath, and second to honor that oath. Clearly no propositional belief is involved in the modern sense. Rather, there is acknowledgment or recognition of known truth, coupled with fidelity. In this sense one could only believe what was known to be true.

An equally striking example is taken from Francis Bacon's 1625 essay, "Of Truth."[4] Bacon describes three relationships a person must have toward truth: "the inquiry of truth," "the knowledge of truth," and the "belief of truth," in that order. He then explains that inquiry is the "wooing of truth," that knowledge is the "presence" of truth, and that belief is "the enjoyment of it." Obviously, belief was not understood strictly as a form of knowing or opinion, but as beloving or cherishing that which was already known to be true.

In both of these illustrations it is vital to see that the opposite of believing the truth is not to be in error, but to lie. To believe a falsehood means to love the lie instead of loving the truth.

Smith traces three major ways in which the meaning of the English word *believe* has undergone almost total reversal in the last 350 years. It once referred to persons, now it refers to statements. People once spoke almost exclusively of their own acts of believing; now we commonly speak of the beliefs of others. Believing used to apply only to what was acknowledged as true and valuable; now it is at least as likely to apply to what is false. Because this transition is as crucial as it is dramatic, Smith pleads with us not to forget that "literally, and originally, 'to believe' means 'to hold dear': virtually, to love."[5]

Faith

A similar transformation has occurred in the meaning of the word *faith*. The Latin word *credo*, for which *faith* is the English equivalent, was formed from the word for heart, combined with a verb suffix meaning "to put." Thus it literally meant to put one's heart into something. More broadly it meant almost exactly the same thing as the English word *believe*—to acknowledge something as true and/or valuable, and to give one's loyalty to it.[6]

The word *faith* retains much of this original meaning in its cognate "faithfulness," and especially in its contrary, "unfaithfulness." These latter words obviously have nothing to do with propositions or opinions. They definitely speak of honor, loyalty, and commitment. To be unfaithful is to violate a vow, commit adultery, practice treason, or abandon a commitment. In the word *faith* itself, however, no doubt because of its close connection with the word *belief,* these primary meanings have been almost overwhelmed by the acquired meaning which has prompted this study. Like *belief,* faith has come to refer to the truth of propositions. One's *faith* is often thought to be the specific doctrines one believes in. And worse yet, it has come to mean believing the truth of propositions for which there is no evidence. Whereas Bacon urged us to enjoy truth known through inquiry, the modern notion of faith often calls us to dogmatically reject inquiry which might challenge our unfounded claims.

The King James Bible

In 1611 the words *faith* and *belief* held virtually the same meaning: to belove, to put one's whole heart into loyalty, commitment, or love of what was known to be true. The consequences of this common meaning for the King James Version of the Bible—and all translations depending on it, including Joseph Smith's "New Translation"—are important. The word *belief* occurs in the KJV only once*, whereas

---

*In fact, the same New Testament Greek word, *pistis,* is translated to read *belief* once, *believe* twice, and *faith* 239 times. The word *pisteuo* is translated *believe* 239 times, and to be *committed* 7 times.

the verb forms of *believe* occur 289 times. The reason seems fairly obvious. The Hebrew and Greek languages, in which the Bible was originally written, have both noun and verb forms for faith, as does Latin, the language of the Christian church and of its translations of the Bible until the Reformation. Wherever possible, therefore, the translators of the KJV preferred the English word *faith* to translate these words. But where a verb was required, in the absence of an English word "faithing" they obviously felt free to use *believe* as a synonym for having faith.

What did the translators of the King James Bible mean by the words *faith* and *belief*? Apparently they did not mean to have an opinion about the truth of some questionable statement. They meant to put one's heart into something, to belove, to acknowledge known truth and to cherish, honor, and be loyal to it.

Obviously, then, given our contemporary understanding of these words, we have been seriously misreading the intention of the English Bible.

Summary

1. The words *faith* and *belief* have undergone a radical transformation in meaning. This transformation has caused many readers of the English Bible to seriously misunderstand the nature of faith.
2. Today the word *believe* commonly means to be of the opinion that a statement is factually correct. A person who does not believe a true statement is said to be in error. Today belief is not fundamentally related to personal loyalty or commitment. Today knowledge displaces belief.
3. Original usage of the English word *believe* most commonly meant belove or obey or something closely related to these. Belief here presupposes knowledge and, therefore, one who does not believe the truth is not mistaken but, rather, loving the lie. This usage deals primarily with values

and is intimately related to personal loyalty and commitment.
4. Given the intimate relationship between faith and belief, a misunderstanding of belief has led to a distorted understanding of faith.
5. Although most biblical passages make sense with either understanding, the sense they make is very different. One understanding connotes opinions, the other values.
6. The English word *faith* is derived from the Latin *credo* which means "to set one's heart." It was originally virtually synonymous with *belief* which meant "to belove." Today, because of the changes undergone by the word *belief* with which it is intimately related, faith has come to refer to the holding of opinions about propositions, usually without or against evidence.
7. While Greek, Hebrew, and Latin all have a verb form of faith, English does not. Since the King James Version of the Bible was written in 1611, before the drastic shifts in meaning, its translators felt free to use *believing* when a verb form was needed for faith.

Study and Discussion Questions

1. Complete the following: The Bible defines *believe* as _____. Today *believe* means _____. Had you known this difference previously or does this come as a surprise to you? How does this insight help you to reunderstand the meaning of faith?
2. Read the following two statements using the word *believe,* then answer the questions below:
   a. I believe in the RLDS church.
   b. I believe in my child.
   How is the word *believe* used in each statement? How is its meaning similar or different?
3. As noted above biblical authors used the word *believe* to mean acceptance of a series of facts

rather than wholehearted love and obedience. How does this affect the way you relate to the gospel? How may this help you face new facts which call into question past understandings that have been part of your beliefs?
4. What benefits or liabilities are there in using the word *faith* to mean what it originally meant—honor, loyalty, putting one's heart into something? In what ways does this usage better enable you to accept the faith of persons who hold differing beliefs from yours?
5. Identify an insight you may have received resulting from your consideration of this chapter.

---

1. *The American Heritage Dictionary of the English Language,* William Morris, ed. (Boston: Houghton Mifflin Co., 1978), 1526.
2. Wilfred Cantwell Smith, *Faith and Belief* (Princeton, New Jersey: Princeton University Press, 1979), 106, 107.
3. *Faith and Belief,* 110.
4. Wilfred Cantwell Smith, *History and Belief* (Charlottesville, Virginia: University Press of Virginia, 1977), 110.
5. *Faith and Belief,* 103.
6. Ibid., chapter 5, especially page 76.

Chapter 14
THE BIBLICAL LANGUAGE OF FAITH AND BELIEF

It seems to be solidly established that the word *believe* as used by the translators of the King James Version of the Bible did not carry the modern meaning of having an opinion about the truth of some statement. Rather it meant to put one's whole heart into something, to cherish, to honor, or to love. The question arises then as to which meaning accurately translates the intention of the biblical texts. How are we supposed to read the Bible where these words appear? Have we been mistaken in thinking that the authors of the Bible called us to assent to the truth of propositions and to believe these propositions without evidence? In this chapter the work of two major biblical scholars on this subject will be summarized. Their results are strikingly similar to the conclusions of W. C. Smith, as described in chapter 13.

One point of caution may be necessary to ward off an unfortunate interpretation of this material. A basic difference exists between what is meant by acknowledgment or recognition in this discussion and the usual modern meaning of belief. Acknowledgment and belief (in the modern sense) both have to do with the truth of statements, and both may be either correct or mistaken. But they are different experiences with different attitudes. We speak of acknowledgment or recognition when we are in a context where the truth in question seems totally obvious or self-evident. We do not merely believe that $2 + 2 = 4$, or that the world is not flat. We must acknowledge these as obvious truths. Nor did the knight referred to in the previous chapter merely believe (have the opinion) that he had made a promise. He knew it was true; and he was being implored to acknowledge that truth. This is different from our usual use of the word *belief* in which we tend to leave some room for doubt or discussion.

History makes it obvious that what seems true to some people at some times does not seem true to others. To the ancient Hebrews it seemed self-evident that the earth was flat and unmoving and that the sun and stars were small lights hung from the sky. Today we know that these views were mistaken. We do not merely believe that they are not true, we know it as confidently as we can know almost anything. So a person who might wish otherwise must still acknowledge the fact that these ancient views were mistaken.

The fact that the ancients were mistaken makes it natural for us to say that they merely believed that the earth stood still while the sun moved. Yet that ignores the vast differences in our situations. For them these views really did seem self-evident. They were confirmed by each rising and setting of the sun. The fact that a few scholars in Greece and Egypt held other views did not affect the world at large.

For most people these views of the world were self-evident truths which were not merely believed, but were assumed and acknowledged.

In the same way the Hebrews assumed the truth of most of their religious views. They were not constantly bombarded by modern historical and scientific evidence to the contrary. We, however, cannot live in modern scientific cultures and escape for long being forced to evaluate and defend our beliefs. Consequently, what the ancient Hebrews could intellectually, emotionally, and ethically see as self-evident truths to be acknowledged may be claims which we have an ethical obligation to examine critically and accept or reject only on the basis of careful reasoning about evidence. We cannot, therefore, simply adopt the content of their biblical faith uncritically. Just because they could acknowledge something as obviously true does not mean that we can. The truth of their assumptions is something we must investigate and not merely assume ourselves.

As we study the biblical view of faith, therefore, we must understand the important intellectual and cultural differences between the authors' world and ours. We should not forget that their situation made it intellectually and ethically reasonable to acknowledge as obvious truth things which we now know to be false. Our knowledge cannot be imposed onto them. They did not merely believe, they knew and acknowledged—even if they were wrong. With this caution about differences, let us turn to an examination of what the early Hebrew writers meant by their words for faith and belief.

Faith and Belief in the Old Testament

The discussion in this section is largely taken from Rudolph Bultmann and Artur Weiser's careful and authoritative study of biblical words for faith and belief.[1]

One preliminary explanation may be helpful. In

their written form, Hebrew words begin with only consonants and then add vowels to vary the root meaning. The basic root form of the word which seems to have been most fundamentally used to express the Old Testament concept of religious faith is 'mn. To this foundation, various combinations of vowels may be added to express different meanings.

The oldest meaning to which Weiser traces this root word is its use in referring to "a child's mother, nurse, attendant."[2] While Weiser cautions that no direct link between this meaning and its eventual transformation into a word for the central religious activity of faith can be proved, the fact of this origin is worth noting. It seems significant because, in the Old Testament, faith is essentially a reciprocal personal relationship between God and persons, one in which God is the initiator.[3] In the Old Testament, faith is attributed not only to persons but also to God:

Know therefore that the Lord your God is God, the faithful God who keeps covenant and steadfast love with those who love him and keep his commandments.—Deuteronomy 7:9 RSV

The same root (*emet* or *emūnā*) which is used to speak of God's faithfulness may be used to mean that God will confirm, establish, or fulfill God's Word and promises. Understood broadly, God's faithfulness is "that which makes God to be God."[4]

Not only is God's Word or promise or law established by faith, however, for faith, as the human response to God's faith, is what establishes human existence in relationship to God and other persons. Isaiah is the principal shaper of this understanding of faith.

It is the problem of how existence is possible, the question of faith and being, which is the center of Isaiah's interest. For Isaiah, faith means an altogether special form of existence for those dependent on God alone, which becomes effective...and forms the foundation laid by God for the divine community (xxxviii. 16). In fact faith and existence are identical for Isaiah.[5]

O Lord, by these things men live, and in all these is the life of my spirit. Oh, restore me to health and make me live!—Isaiah 38:16 RSV

The Jerusalem Bible's translation of this passage is especially powerful.

Lord, my heart will live for you, my spirit will live for you alone. You will cure me and give me life, my suffering will turn to health. It is you who have kept my soul from the pit of nothingness, you have thrust all of my sins behind your back.—Isaiah 38:16, 17 JB

What, then, is the nature and content of this faith which establishes our existence in relationship to God? Faith is twofold: it is acknowledgment or recognition, coupled with wholehearted commitment. That is, we must acknowledge that God is God and that God has already established a relationship with humankind, and then choose to put ourselves totally into that relationship. "The phrase *with all your heart and with all your soul,* of which Deuteronomy is particularly fond (df. Deut. vi. 5 *et passim*), leaves no doubt how the OT [Old Testament] wishes the attitude of faith to be understood."[6]

Hear, O Israel: The Lord our God is one Lord; and you shall love the Lord your God with all your heart, and with all your soul, and with all your might.—Deuteronomy 6:4, 5 RSV

In contrast to this, Hosea 10:2 condemns those whose heart is "divided" (JB and Weiser) or "false" (RSV).

It is interesting to note that the word *amen* derives from the root 'mn. (amen)...includes both the subjective (theoretical) knowledge and recognition, and also at the same time the practical submission of the whole person with his understanding, will and attitude to the obligations of the command (or curse, or doxology) in question. Thus the term 'mn, when used in this form, comprises a double reference: the knowledge and recognition of the relation between the obligation and its realization, and the fact that this obligation with all its practical consequences is binding on him who says *Amen.*[7]

A little reflection will show that the word *amen* still carries this double reference of acknowledgment and commitment. When someone says something which we recognize to be true and to which we commit ourselves, we may well feel compelled to declare, "Amen!" And, of course, it is still the word with which we close all prayers, acknowledging and affirming our relationship to the One to whom we pray.

The various meanings of the word *believe* are also extremely important for our considerations. The word may be formed from different consonant roots and may be combined with different grammatical forms in order to express different meanings. Some of these roots are very much like our modern sense of belief but coupled with an attitude. "Thus in profane usage *to believe* a word, a report, a piece of news, means first to be aware of and to accept as true the thing reported, but at the same time it includes an attitude appropriate to the thing reported."[8]

One form of *to believe* (*he emin*) is built from the root 'mn and carries essentially the same meanings as the word *faith*. This form "can be defined...most simply as saying Amen to something with all the consequences for the subject and the object." In this form the word emphasizes "the basic attitude which is associated in English with the word 'trust.'" It acknowledges a claim inherent in a relationship. "Moreover the Old Testament uses it only for a personal relationship; for also behind the word which is trusted there stands the man who is trusted."[9]

Thus, when the Old Testament uses this term to denote a person's relationship to God, the term basically means that the person "says Amen to God." Further, *to believe* "appears as a formal term signifying to recognize and to acknowledge the relationship into which God enters with man, i.e., to put oneself into this relationship. Thus here too the reciprocal relationship between God and man is part of the essence of faith."[10] "When a command, order, or commandment is concerned (Deut. ix. 23, Ps. cxix. 66 [II Kings xvii. 14]), then faith means the acknowledgment of the demand and man's obedience. When attention is concentrated on God's praises (Genesis xv.

6. [Ps cvi. 12]), then [this form of *to believe*] expresses the acknowledgment of the promise and of the power of God to perform it, and includes the honoring of God as the mighty Lord (Num. xx. 12)."[11]

Since *to believe* in this form means to acknowledge and trust, not to believe often means to become apostate. It is especially used in this sense to refer to the refusal to accept God's promises, the failure to respond to God's saving deeds, and unfaithfulness to God's covenant. Primarily, unbelief would refer to a person's or community's separation from the sacral covenant, or, as indicated earlier, a failure to commit oneself wholeheartedly to the covenant or to God.

While other forms of the word *to believe* are commonly used with reference to other gods and idols, this special form derived from 'mn is never used in that context.[12] Even if a Hebrew had been of the opinion that gods other than Yahweh existed, the Old Testament would not speak of that person as believing in those gods. Weiser points out that since believing in this special sense is a wholehearted commitment, and since one cannot give oneself wholeheartedly to many gods at the same time, it necessarily follows that this belief is monotheistic.

This use of the word *believe* obviously has very little in common with most of the modern English forms of that word. It does not mean to have an opinion, whether firm or weak, true or false; for it is not an opinion at all, but a way of being in relationship to persons or God. This form of belief is virtually identical with faith.

Summary

1. We "acknowledge" or "recognize" in contexts where the truth seems obvious or self-evident. We "believe" when there is some room for doubt. What seems self-evident in one historical context may not seem so in others. Therefore, religious views deemed by biblical authors to be

self-evident truths which should be acknowledged must not necessarily be seen as such by modern persons. Given the vast differences in cultural contexts between the modern world and that of biblical authors, we must not accept the beliefs of biblical authors uncritically.

2. In the Old Testament, faith is essentially a reciprocal relationship between God and persons—a relationship in which God is the initiator. Faith is attributed not only to persons but also to God. God's essential nature is God's faithfulness.

3. In the Old Testament, faith, as the human response to God's faith, is what establishes human existence in relationship to God and other persons.

4. Old Testament faith consists of acknowledging God and the relationship God has established with persons and choosing to give wholehearted commitment to that relationship.

5. The word *amen* derives from the same Hebrew root (*'mn*) as the word *faith* (*emet*) and carries a similar doubled-edged meaning of acknowledgment and commitment.

6. Old Testament belief consists not only of accepting as true, but also of developing an attitude concerning, and appropriate to, that which is accepted.

7. One form of the Hebrew word for *to believe* (*he emin*) in the Old Testament is derived from the same root as *faith* and emphasizes the attitude of trust. This form is reserved for personal relationships and means saying amen to that relationship; that is, it means to acknowledge and trust. This form is never used in reference to other gods or idols and must entail monotheism.

8. In the Old Testament, not to believe means, primarily, to become apostate. It describes a person's or community's separation from the rela-

tionship to God or the failure to give wholehearted commitment to the relationship or to God.

Study and Discussion Questions

1. What is the meaning of the following?
   Acknowledgment means _____.
   Belief means _____.
   How are they different or the same? How does this affect your study of biblical faith?
2. What is your reaction to the view that faith as seen in the Old Testament is also an attribute of God? Does this come as a surprise to you? Why or why not?
3. What does the author identify as the twofold nature of faith?

   _____

   _____

4. In your opinion, is it easier to put your faith—"With all your heart and with all your soul"—into beliefs or into relationships? Why?
5. Briefly review the author's discussion of the word *amen*. For him the word means _____.
   What is your definition of *amen*? How are your definition and the author's similar or different in meaning?
6. The author discusses the nature of the Hebrew use of *belief* as monotheistic. Do you agree that people need to return to the early use of the word (commitment to something) rather than continue the present use (assent to propositions)? How is this usage consistent or inconsistent with current use of the word? Why or why not?
7. What have you learned from studying this chapter?

   _____

   _____

Specific Scriptures Suggested for Careful Study

When trying to understand the scriptures, nothing can replace direct study of the text. Learning to read them with the original meaning of *faith* and *believe* will require practice. Unfortunately, most scriptures will make sense with both the old and new meanings, but the sense they make is very different.

Consider, for example, Psalm 119. The entire psalm is in praise of God's law. The psalmist speaks of his reverence for and obedience to the Law as the perfect guide to life. In verse 66 he speaks of believing God's commandments. A little thought will show that since commands (Close the door! Give me the key! Thou shalt not kill!) are neither true nor false, it makes no logical sense to believe them in the modern sense. But it makes perfect sense to believe them in the sense of acknowledging and obeying.

The following scriptures will reward careful study. In most cases one of the key words under study will occur, but all of these passages say something important about the attitude which the Bible advocates. Ask yourself in each case how the meaning of the text changes when you use the old and new senses of *belief* and *faith*. You should also study them in more than one version. Only in Genesis 15:1-6 does the Inspired Version offer change of any significance. In that case, readers are encouraged to make use of modern Bibles like the Revised Standard Version, the Jerusalem Bible, the New American Bible and the New English Bible for comparison. Notice that the Revised Standard Version keeps the King James Version's use of *believe* while the others frequently substitute words like "rely," "trust," and "venerated," which, as we have seen, more accurately reflect the original sense of the text.

Isaiah 43:10. Notice that knowing comes before believing.

Psalm 78, especially verse 32, and also II Kings

17:1-13. These passages provide excellent examples of the biblical assumption that the "evidence" available to the Hebrews was overwhelming. Faith is not "belief without evidence"! Rather, the opposite of belief is rebellion, knowing rebellion.

Exodus 14:30, 31.

Numbers 14:11.

Deuteronomy 1:26-32; 9:23, 24.

Psalm 106:7-12.

Psalm 119. Compare verse 66 with verses 10, 14, 15, 34-6, 48, 69, et. al.

Genesis 15:1-6 (1-9 in the Inspired Version. Note that the Inspired Version has significant changes here.)

John 8:42-55 clearly identifies believing with loving the truth.

Romans 1:19-25 and 2:6-8. Paul insists the existence of God is self-evident even to the heathen. Failure to obey God is a result of sin, not lack of evidence. (The wording of the Inspired Version is slightly different, but I do not think it changes the meaning.)

II Thessalonians 2:9-13. Read carefully, this clearly identifies *belief* with love of the truth.

James 2, especially verse 19. This is an unusual passage where the use of *believe* is almost modern. But careful thought will show that (1) "the devils" would certainly not lack for evidence, and (2) what makes them "devils" is precisely that they know the truth about God but still refuse to acknowledge and obey God. When this is put in the context of James' emphatic plea that "faith without works is dead," it is obvious that for James, faith must not be reduced to mere belief.

Hebrews 11. This is a key passage, keeping Romans 1 in mind. Like Paul, the author assumes that the truth of God is self-evident to those who love the truth.

1. Rudolph Bultmann, and Artur Weiser, *Faith* (London: Adam and Charles Black, 1961).
2. Ibid., 3, see also 11 n3.
3. Ibid., 3, 9, 12, and elsewhere.
4. Ibid., 7, 8.
5. Ibid., 15, 16.
6. Ibid., 14.
7. Ibid., 9, 10.
8. Ibid., 10.
9. Ibid., 11.
10. Ibid., 11.
11. Ibid., 12.
12. Ibid., 15.

Chapter 15
IMPLICATIONS: BIBLICAL FAITH AND MODERN BELIEF

Linguistically, the claim of the preceding chapter is rather simple and clearly demonstrable. The meanings of the words *believe* and *faith* have changed. They used to mean that a person acknowledged and loved. They included such meanings as loyalty, commitment, and obedience. Today the word *believe* primarily means to hold an opinion, while the word *faith,* though more divided, often means to hold that opinion without evidence. For the sake of communication, the word *faith* in this chapter will be used to convey its original meaning, and the word *belief* to convey the meaning which it actually has in modern usage.

The claim about language is expressed in a radical form by W. C. Smith when, as observed earlier, he asserts that "belief, in the modern meaning of the word, has had no place in the history of Christian thought. *The concept is not in the Bible.*"[1] Whether this is true without qualification is a question which can only be resolved by much more work. But it should be obvious that it is at least substantially correct. As a historian of religions, Smith goes on to make a related but even more radical claim:

The idea that believing is religiously important turns out to be a modern idea. It has arisen in recent times, in ways that can be ascertained and demonstrated.... A great modern heresy of the Church is the heresy of believing. Not of believing this or that, but of believing as such. The view that to believe is of central significance—this is an aberration.[2]

Such a shocking claim requires careful explanation. It is not that persons who wrote or were written about in the Bible had no beliefs, no opinions. What Smith is correctly asserting is that having an opinion about the truth of certain propositions about the world and religion was not the central religious attitude advocated by the Bible. What we, as modern readers, tend to see as problems of belief were, for them, assumptions calling for response.

There are two elements to this claim. First, biblical scholars and historians are in strong agreement that, in general, ancient people, for a variety of reasons, were not as concerned about objectivity and proof as are modern Westerners. The ancient notion of history, for example, did not include the demand for objectivity and careful documentation that we make upon modern historians (let alone news reporters). While we cannot know about that for which we have no record, the Bible reflects none of the interest in natural science which was so prevalent in the work of Greek philosophers from the same periods. It is not legitimate to respond that the Hebrews may have had such interest but that it naturally was not recorded in the religious writings, for that is the whole point. They did not view such issues, if they addressed them at all, as religiously significant.

Second, whether or not the Hebrews addressed questions of natural science and philosophy, it is obvious that they had an entirely different point of view regarding the world than do we. While ancient cultures had some students of nature, they were not scientific cultures. Generally speaking, ancient peoples had no way to account for the world through natural process; there was no concept of natural law in Hebrew thought. When confronted with growing crops, falling rain, changing seasons, lightning, thunder, or the rising of the sun, they could only respond, "God did it." No other answer was available. In the absence of alternative explanations, the reality and power of an invisible creator or creators would have seemed self-evident.

Ancient Hebrews were not constantly confronted by scientific and historical challenges to their views of the world and God. They were free to assume that the world was flat with a dome over it, that spirits caused disease, and that God caused the sun to rise. The fact that we know they were mistaken is irrelevant. They were able to treat all of these as simple, unchallenged truths. For this same reason they could simply assume that Yahweh had created Adam from the mud, had led Israel through the sea, and had stopped the motion of the sun. These were not beliefs to be held against the evidence; they were accepted as historical assumptions. Consequently, questions of factual truth were not part of most of their religious inquiry. The central issue was, "Given these assumed truths, where will you put your heart?"

An illustration may help. If I were trying to decide whether to marry someone, I would not be centrally concerned with settling factual claims about that person. I already know the person well and am free to assume the basic truth of my view of that person. The fundamental question of marriage is not factual. The question is, given all of these acknowledged facts, do I love that person and choose to commit my life to that love?

In just the same way, the authors of the Bible generally accepted the truth of their natural and religious views. For them the central question was not about belief, but about faith. "Faith in the OT [Old Testament] is thus a moral response, not the acceptance of ideas or dogmas about God."[3] The question of faith was whether people were willing to acknowledge the truth about God and love God.

How does this affect our use of the Bible in modern discussions on the nature of faith? In answering this we must use great caution in distinguishing the *nature* of faith from the *content* of faith.

Many readers may be strongly tempted to simply adopt the biblical view uncritically. They may claim that faith means believing in the existence of God and the divinity of Christ, that these are self-evident truths, and that anyone who fails to hold them does so out of sheer perversity. In fact, this is exactly the view which many people do have. But we cannot simply transfer the *content* of biblical faith into the modern discussion in the same way that we may transfer the concept of the *nature* of faith.

The content of the biblical faith included a primitive world view—a view of the world as flat with a dome over it within which were stored the rain, hail, and snow. The primitive world view involved no possibility of natural explanation for events. Little imagination is needed to understand why the ancient Hebrews were able to see the flatness of the earth as a self-evident truth which no sensible person would deny. Thus they were able to acknowledge as true something we now know to be false. This alone should give us grounds for caution about transferring their religious assumptions into the modern world.

If we cannot uncritically transfer the content of biblical faith into the modern world, what can we draw from the Bible? We can draw an understanding of the nature of faith which is powerfully relevant to our modern world. This can be divided into two parts.

First, faith is loving commitment to that which we recognize as being of ultimate value. This is surely true to the biblical writers' intention. They saw Yahweh as the one being who deserved their ultimate love and obedience. We may or may not share their beliefs about the nature of that ultimate value. We may think of God as a supreme being or we may think of God in other terms. Whatever we value ultimately, that we will call God, and to that we will give our faith.

Second, we will remember that the biblical notion of faith involved the acknowledgment and love of truth. In the modern world we may be much less able to feel confident that we know the truth. The scientist, for example, is never ultimately committed to any particular hypothesis. Yet there can still be an ultimate commitment to that quest for ever greater understanding of the truth. In the modern world, that quest means a deep loyalty to the demands of logic and evidence, the means by which we discover truth. This kind of love of the truth is well described by the philosopher John Locke in *An Essay Concerning Human Understanding:*

He that would seriously set upon the search of truth, ought in the first place to prepare his mind with a love of it. For he that loves it not, will not take much pains to get it; nor be much concerned when he misses it. There is nobody in the commonwealth of learning who does not profess himself a lover of truth: and there is not a rational creature that would not take it amiss to be thought otherwise of. And yet, for all this, one may truly say, that there are very few lovers of truth, for truth's sake, even amongst those who persuade themselves they are so. How a man may know whether he be so in earnest, is worth inquiry: and I think there is one unerring mark of it, viz. The not entertaining any proposition with greater assurance than the proofs it is built upon will warrant.[4]

Stated simply, a modern faith must be one which

includes a loyalty to the search for truth, a loyalty which will require us to abandon even our most cherished beliefs when the evidence demands it. We will not hold on to traditional beliefs when they are not supported by evidence. We will not make a virtue of belief without evidence. Modern faith, as acknowledgment of and loyalty to the quest for truth by reason and evidence, is the exact antithesis of belief without evidence.

These two elements of faith are not in conflict with each other. If we are ultimately committed to God, then we will naturally want to know the truth about God so that we may express that commitment as effectively as possible. We will also want to know the truth about the people we are called to love and the world in which we are to work. We cannot be ultimately committed to something and still refuse to inquire into the true nature of that which we value. Thus the ultimate love of God and the ultimate love of truth are not in conflict with each other. As the authors of the Bible recognized, the only true faith is the faith which is willing to acknowledge the truth and obey it.

Nor is the demand for reason and evidence in conflict with appeals to the heart. It is irrational to forget that feelings are often irrational. Our passion cannot and should not be replaced by cold calculation, but neither should we allow emotions to displace responsible intelligence. Maturity and wisdom involve learning to let reason and passion contribute in their own appropriate ways to the wholeness of human life.

An Example: World View

An example of this point should help to eliminate the possibility of misunderstanding. Persons living in the scientific culture of the modern Western world cannot simply adopt the unscientific, uncritical view of the world held by the authors of the Bible. To do so is to refuse to acknowledge truths which we have that they lacked.

The authors of the Bible, though never discussing it directly, clearly assumed that the world was flat and had a dome over it which kept out the primordial waters which surrounded the earth. The Hebrews knew of no other world but this one. They had no language to distinguish the earth from some larger universe. This flat world, with sun, moon, and stars hung from the dome like lanterns was, according to Genesis 1, constructed in six days. This is evident to a careful reader of that story. The firmament which divides the waters above from the waters below is not earth but "heaven" (Genesis 1:7, 8 or IV 1:10, 11). The word translated "firmament" is really a word meaning "a strip of beaten metal."[5] (In Job 37:18, however, the sky is described as being "hard as a molten mirror.") Into this firm, hard dome the lights of heaven are set. (See the illustration.)

In such a world the imagery of the book of Revelation makes sense. Given such a view of the heavenly realm, it is appropriate to say that "the sun became black as sackcloth, the full moon became like blood, and the stars of the sky fell to the earth as the fig tree sheds its winter fruit when shaken by a gale; the sky vanished like a scroll that is rolled up" (Revelation 6:12-14 RSV). Elsewhere the author can imagine a great red dragon so tall that its tail beat against the dome and "swept down a third of the stars of heaven" (Revelation 12:3, 4 RSV). Since in such a world, rain is caused by opening the windows of heaven to let the waters above fall through (Genesis 7:11, 8:2, IV 8:36, 48), it makes sense to say that God's witnesses "have power to shut the sky, that no rain may fall" (Revelation 11:6 RSV).

It is hardly surprising that the ancient Hebrews should have thought of the world in this way, and that it would even have seemed self-evident to them. Perhaps you can remember your own images of the

THE HEBREW CONCEPTION OF THE UNIVERSE

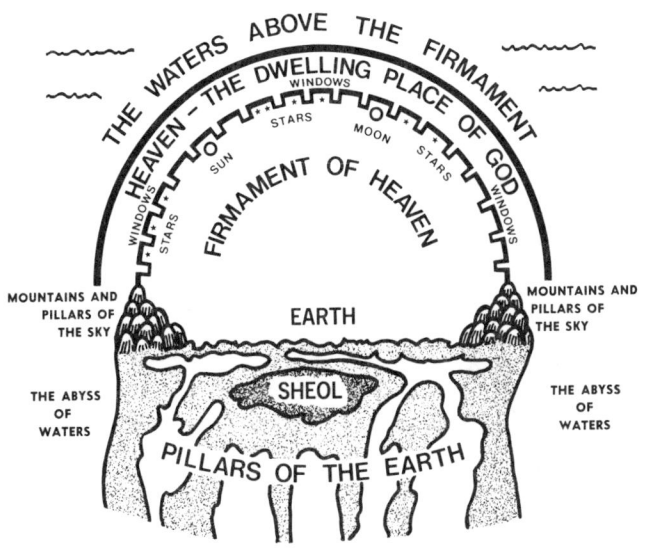

THE HEBREW CONCEPTION OF THE UNIVERSE ASSUMED A FLAT EARTH SUPPORTED OVER A WATERY ABYSS. A SOLID FIRMAMENT HELD BACK THE WATERS ABOVE THE EARTH AND TO IT WERE ATTACHED THE HEAVENLY BODIES. AT THE OUTERMOST LIMITS OF EARTH A CIRCULAR RANGE OF MOUNTAINS SUPPORTED THE FIRMAMENT.

world when you were a small child listening to the lullaby:

Twinkle, twinkle little star, how I wonder what you are,
Up above the world so high, like a candle in the sky.

The inside cover of one of the science books on my shelf has a print of a man who has climbed the mountain range which supports a dome, and is sticking his head through to see what lies beyond. Such images are natural in a prescientific culture or mind. The flatness of the earth and the dome of the sky have almost certainly been seen by most of the people during the history of the earth as obvious truths which only a fool could doubt.

Our children today grow up watching television cartoons of rocket ships traveling to distant suns and planets. They see pictures of the earth taken from the moon. They see the space shuttle take off into space and send back pictures of the world from 150 miles above. Thus even though we still speak of the sun rising and setting, and of the sky as high, our children and we know that the biblical view of the world is mistaken. This is not mere belief, but an incontrovertible truth which we must acknowledge.

Once we recognize that the ancient Hebrews held this prescientific view of the world, it should follow that we will stop expecting them to have an accurate scientific account of the origin of the world. The world created in six days is not the world in which we live. It is terrible mistake to insist that because the authors of the Bible held such a view we have some moral or religious obligation to hold it, too. Such an insistence says that we must refuse to acknowledge the truth which we can now see, and to love the error rather than the truth. If we adopt the biblical understanding of the nature of faith, we must automatically abandon some of the content of biblical faith. Because to acknowledge and love the truth means to accept the evidence which confronts us daily. Clearly, insistence on what is called special creation is a violation of the biblical understanding of the nature of faith, even though it is a partial adherence to biblical views of the world. (Note that a full adherence to those views would require us to believe that the world had a dome over it.)

The Bible contains profound witness to human history and experience. It is the foundational document of the Judaic-Christian tradition, telling us of our origins. Yet in many respects, loving the truth today involves different beliefs and different acknowledgments than it did two thousand years ago. We cannot love the truth if we refuse to recognize that past or current beliefs may be false. Such a refusal to grow in knowledge is a direct rejection of the biblical notion of the nature of faith. Thus scientists who work with hypotheses, always being open to new insight even when it overthrows previously cherished theories, are actually working out of a biblical approach to faith as the love of truth rather than the love of the lie. The same is true of historians, biblical scholars, and ourselves. When we love our own cherished views about the world, or God, or Christ, or the scriptures, more than we love the truth about them, we violate the Bible's understanding of the nature of faith.

Summary

1. Today the word *belief* primarily means opinion, and the word *faith* often means to hold that opinion without any supporting evidence.
2. Wilfred Cantwell Smith asserts that having an opinion about the truth of propositions was not the central religious attitude of the authors of the Bible. They dealt primarily with acknowledgment and commitment to self-evident truths, not withholding opinions about dubious matters. This is partly because ancient peoples were not as concerned about objectivity and proof as are modern Westerners. Also, due to their world

view and the absence of concepts of natural process, the reality of God was self-evident as that which created and managed the world. The question of faith was then "given the reality of God, does one choose to love and commit oneself to God?"

3. We must not uncritically accept the *content* of biblical faith—beliefs produced by a primitive world view—into our modern lives the way that we can adopt insights gained about the *nature* of biblical faith. Adoption of the biblical understanding of the nature of faith forces us to abandon part of the content of the biblical faith. We cannot love the truth and refuse to recognize that some past or current beliefs are inadequate.

4. The biblical nature of faith, highly relevant for us today, can be divided into two parts. First, faith is loving commitment to that which we recognize as being of ultimate value. Second, faith involves a commitment to the truth. This commitment today involves the abandonment of even a most cherished belief when the evidence demands that it no longer adequately expresses the reality of the object of faith.

5. The ultimate love of God and the ultimate love of truth are in perfect harmony with one another.

Study and Discussion Questions

1. What is the radical claim about the modern use of the word belief in religion, as made by W. C. Smith? How does the author consider and discuss this claim? Do you agree or disagree with it? Why?
2. How did early Hebrews view the need for objectivity and proof, two strong concerns for modern day Westerners?
3. The scripture references found on page 188 depict various characteristics and assumptions

about the Hebrew universe (see diagram, page 189). Based on the discussion in the chapter, select several of these scriptures and study them. Then review the author's discussion of this world view on pages 190-191. Why do you agree or disagree with the author's view?

  A. Why does it make sense not to expect the Hebrews to have an accurate scientific account of the origin of the world?
  B. Is an insistence on viewing literally the biblical account of creation a refusal to acknowledge the known facts, and thus, to love the error rather than the truth? Why or why not?
  C. Why is a willingness to grow in knowledge (by accepting a modern world view) not a direct rejection of the biblical notion of faith's nature? Do you agree or disagree with the author's view and why?

4. What is your response to the author's statement that "we cannot simply transfer the *content* of biblical faith into the modern discussion in the same way that we may transfer the concept of the *nature* of faith" (page 185)? Why do you think he says this? In your estimation, which element is it most important to transfer? Why?

5. Into what two parts does the author divide the biblical nature of faith?

_____

_____

6. Why is it important not to hold onto traditional beliefs without any evidence? What is your view and why? What reason would you give to support your view?

7. Why is it important not to replace passion with cold calculation, and intelligence with emotions?

For what reason might it be important to "let reason and passion contribute in their own appropriate ways to the wholeness of human life"?
8. What is your reaction to the author's statement that "it is a terrible mistake to insist that because the authors of the Bible held such a view [flat earth covered with a dome] we have some moral or religious obligation to hold it too"? What is gained from holding such a view today? What is harmful about it? Why?
9. Have you received any new understandings while studying the material in this chapter? If so, what are they?

———————————————————————

———————————————————————

---

1. W. C. Smith, *Belief and History* (Charlottesville: University of Virginia Press, 1977), 78.
2. Ibid., Preface.
3. E. C. Backman, "Faith," *Interpreter's Dictionary of the Bible* (Nashville: Abingdon Press, 1962), 2:255.
4. John Locke, *An Essay Concerning Human Understanding* (New York: Dover Publications, 1959), 2, chapter 19.
5. T. H. Gaster, "Firmament," *Interpreter's Dictionary of the Bible* (Nashville: Abingdon Press, 1962), 2:270.

THE HEBREW UNIVERSE: REFERENCES
1. Genesis 1:1-10, 14-17 (IV 1:3-14, 18-20). Firmament divides water above and below; firmament is heaven.
2. I Samuel 2:8. World set on pillars.
3. Job 37:18. Spread out sky hard as molten looking glass.
4. Psalm 19:6. God goes to the end of heaven.
5. Job 22:14. God walks circuit of heaven.
6. Psalm 104:2-3. Heavens stretched like curtain. Lays beams of his chambers in the waters. Clouds his chariots. Walks on wings of wind.
7. Ezekiel 1:26. Throne on firmament, a human sits on it in likeness of God.
8. Genesis 7:11-8:2 (IV 8:36, 48). Fountains of deep broken, windows opened.
9. Psalm 78:23. God opens doors of heaven to make it rain.

10. Psalm 148:4. Waters above heavens.
11. Job 37:10. By breath of God frost is given.
12. Job 26:7. God hangs the earth upon nothing.
13. Job 38:4-7. Where were you when I laid the foundations of the earth?
14. Revelation 11:1; 6:12-14; 12:3, 4.
15. *The Twentieth Century Bible Commentary*, page 542.
16. *Oxford Annotated Bible* (RSV), see especially annotations for Genesis 1:2. (IV 1:4), 1:6-8 (IV 9-11), 7:11 (IV 8:36), 3:6, 2:10-14; Job 26:7, 38:4-7; Proverbs 3:19, 20, 8:28.
17. Paul Heinish, *History of the Old Testament*, page 13.
18. *Abingdon Bible Commentary*, pages 126, 7 under cosmogony; Hebrew cosmology page 783a; Old Testament page 170a; primitive page 527a. Also heaven.
19. *New Catholic Encyclopedia*, under cosmogony, Volume 4.
20. *The Interpreter's Dictionary of the Bible*, under "earth"; "heaven"; "cosmogony"; and "firmament."

Part V

FURTHER THOUGHTS

Chapter 16
THE CREATIVE ROLE OF DOUBT IN RELIGION*

A college student approached his professor after class. With anguish he complained, "I don't know whether you know it or not, but this class is painful." "How's that?" the professor asked. "Well," the student continued, "you have convinced me that we ought to do what you are encouraging us to do, but when I do what you suggest, it's so painful."

What had this professor suggested? What had he encouraged his students to do, the doing of which created, in at least one student, pain? He had encouraged them to doubt creatively. That is, he had

---

*The first part of this chapter is a reprint of "The Creative Role of Doubt in Religion" by Robert M. Baird, Professor of Philosophy, Baylor University, Waco, Texas, found in the *Journal of Religion and Health*, Volume 19, Number 3, Fall 1980, Human Sciences Press, pages 172-179. Used by permission.

encouraged his students to challenge and evaluate the fundamental values—ethical, political, and religious—to which they were committed. At first glance, it may seem as if anyone who would sanction, much less encourage, such activity is an intellectual cynic determined to create psychological chaos. Before such a judgment is rendered, however, attention should be given to the nature of creative doubt and to the reasons that can be advanced in its defense. That is the purpose of this essay.

These arguments are intended, however, to be taken within a certain framework or context. The context can be made clear by contrasting the situations of two individuals, one historical and one fictional. The historical figure is Socrates. The fictional character is St. Emmanuel, the protagonist of Miguel de Unamuno's short work, "St. Emmanuel the Good, Martyr."

Concerning Socrates, recall the cardinal principle he defended at his trial, as that trial is recounted in Plato's *Apology*. The unexamined life, he argued, is not worth living. By this claim Socrates meant that to be a rational human being is to have a kind of creative doubt about one's fundamental value beliefs, a creative doubt that promotes, within reason, a continual reappraisal of such beliefs. This Socratic attitude is vividly illustrated in the dialogue *Euthyphro*. Socrates encounters the young Euthyphro on the porch of the courthouse early one morning. In response to Socrates' query about why he is there, Euthyphro replies that he is in the process of prosecuting his own father and adds that the act of bringing his father to account is itself an act of great piety. At that point Socrates commends Euthyphro for his courage and wisdom and for the piety that he claims. By the way, asks Socrates, what is piety anyway? And with the question Socrates opens the way for a lengthy conversation in which it is revealed that Euthyphro is quite confused about what genuine piety comes to, even though he is prosecuting his father precisely because he thinks to do so is an act of piety. In the process Euthyphro is challenged to rethink some of his most fundamental ideas. This dialogue and this incident are very revealing of the activity of Socrates. He viewed himself as a gadfly with a god-given task of stimulating men to think, to evaluate critically the fundamental principles in terms of which they were structuring their lives. There is an ethics of belief, Socrates would have argued. And one is morally justified in holding a belief only to the extent that it can be justified after critical assessment. Consequently, he not only sanctioned but openly stimulated creative doubt.

Consider, on the other hand, St. Emmanuel, Unamuno's creation. Emmanuel was parish priest of the small, rural village of Valverde de Lucerna. His story is told by his only two educated parishioners, Angela Carballino and her brother Lazarus. Angela describes Emmanuel: "How he did love his people! His life consisted in salvaging wrecked marriages, in forcing unruly sons to submit to their parents, or reconciling parents to their sons, and above all, of consoling the embittered and the weary in spirit; meanwhile he helped everyone to die well."[1] "The priest's effect on people was such that everyone confessed themselves to him without the need of a confessional."[2] "When it came to dying...most of the villagers refused to die unless they were holding on to Don Emmanuel's hand, as if to an anchor chain."[3]

Eventually Angela's brother Lazarus comes to understand that Emmanuel, upon whom the villagers depend so thoroughly, no longer believes certain religious doctrines that have provided for his parishioners such peace and happiness. When Lazarus encourages Emmanuel to proclaim the truth as he sees it, Emmanuel responds: "The Truth? The truth, Lazarus, is perhaps something so unbearable, so terrible, something so deadly, that simple people could not live with it!"[4] Committed to the proposition that the happiness of his parishioners is the ultimate value, Emmanuel argues that "it's better for them to believe everything, even things that contradict one another, than to believe nothing. The idea that someone who believes too much ends by not believing in anything is a Protestant notion. Let us not protest! Protestation destroys contentment and peace."[5] The case he makes for his point of view is so persuasive that eventually even Angela and Lazarus judge him to be a saint among saints and a genuine martyr.

Here we have, then, an age-old conflict. Socrates versus Emmanuel. Truth versus happiness. And the reason it is an age-old conflict is precisely because the competing claims of the two values—truth and contentment—are both so compelling.

When, in fact, the values of truth and happiness *are* in conflict, that is, when the truth is painful or when happiness is dependent upon refusing to pursue the truth, surely the value taking priority depends upon the nature of the situation. This opens the door for a possible resolution of the suggested conflict between Socrates and Emmanuel.

Socrates, one might argue with considerable plausibility, was addressing his "the unexamined life is not worth living" remarks to students, teachers (i.e., the traveling sophists), and the political leaders of Athens. Emmanuel, on the other hand, makes clear that he is concerned with the wellbeing of the simple, uneducated people of his rural village. And what one does, for example, in the classroom with students who have paid their money ostensibly to be stimulated to think and what one does in conversation with a ninety-five-year-old grandmother whose dogmatic and inconsistent religious views are her abiding source of joy and comfort are surely two different things. All of this is to say that the following arguments are in defense of stimulating creative doubt in certain contexts, while acknowledging that there are other settings in which such activity would be inappropriate.

Consider, then, four arguments in defense of creative doubt.

Acknowledging Human Limitations

First, creative doubt is a means of constructively acknowledging human limitations. The American pragmatist Charles Sanders Peirce addressed himself to this issue in terms of his doctrine of Fallibilism.[6] This view states simply that with regard to matters of fact human beings are fallible; they can never be absolutely certain that they are correct. "This," observes Peirce, "is my conclusion, after many years study of the logic of science."[7] The scientist recognizes his limitations and, at most, claims a greater or lesser degree of probability for his conclusions. The implication here is that science has made the progress it has precisely because of a methodology that acknowledges limitations and therefore, encourages reevaluation of conclusions. Acknowledging the possibility that he might be mistaken, the scientist stands prepared to alter his beliefs in the light of new evidence. Should the philosopher or theologian, asks Peirce, be less sensitive to *his* fallibility, less prepared to alter *his* beliefs if reason and evidence warrant? No knowledge claim, concludes Peirce, is ever absolute but "always swims, as it were, in a continuum of uncertainty and indeterminacy."[8] Such an epistemological conclusion is an inevitable corollary of human fallibility.

In this context, consider the notion of faith. What has just been said concerning the possible fallibility of any given human belief is relevant to an understanding of faith. To be sure, belief and faith are not identical, but belief is involved in faith. Paul Tillich's analysis of faith as "the state of being ultimately concerned"[9] is widely held. It must be emphasized, however, that ultimate concern is always intentional: that is, if one is ultimately concerned, one is ultimately concerned about something. Faith, then, is wholly committing oneself to that which one believes to be of ultimate value. Tillich himself argues that "it must be stated as sharply and insistently as possible that in every act of faith there is cognitive affirmation."[10] But where there is cognitive affirmation, there is the possibility of error due to human limitations. And, again, Tillich has forcefully insisted that doubt is a part of the very structure of faith.[11]

Care must be taken, however, in what one attributes to Tillich. He distinguishes in *Dynamics of Faith* between methodological doubt (the kind of humility Peirce associates with the scientific method), skeptical doubt ("an attitude of actually rejecting any certainty"[12]), and existential doubt. It is the latter that Tillich explicitly claims is an essential dimension of faith. In fact, and despite his disclaimers, Tillich's actual discussion of the dynamics of faith suggests that methodological and skeptical doubt are also inherent in faith. For to the extent that faith involves cognitive affirmation, to that extent methodological and skeptical doubt also should be seen as part of the structure of faith. The very fact that faith can be misplaced, that is, that one can take as ultimate that which is not ultimate at all, is a reflection of the logical possibility that a person may be mistaken. Even if one refers to his ultimate concern as "God," humility insists upon the question: Does one's understanding of God correspond to reality? Creative doubt encourages this question. Dogmatism suppresses it.

In connection with this proposition that creative doubt is a means of acknowledging human finitude, a segment from Bronowski's film series "The Ascent of Man" comes vividly to mind. In the final scene of the film "Knowledge or Certainty," Bronowski wades out into a muddy stream at the Auschwitz prison camp. Kneeling down, he scoops up a handful of mud from the very pond into which were flushed the ashes of some four million people. Reflecting upon what men do to one another when they are absolutely and dogmatically certain that they are right and have the final answer, Bronowski pleads with the film audience in the words of Oliver Cromwell: "I beseech you, in the bowels of Christ, think it possible you may be mistaken."[13] The point is, creative doubt is a constructive expression of the recognition that one is not God and, therefore, just may be mistaken.

Keeping Fundamental Beliefs Alive

A second argument stresses that creative doubt can play a role in keeping one's fundamental beliefs from becoming dead dogmas.

Most basic beliefs and value commitments are initially inherited from parents, peers, and society at large. If these beliefs and commitments are not challenged by creative doubt, they tend to become simply verbal professions having little vitality. Creative doubt stimulates the evaluation of beliefs. Beliefs found wanting may appropriately be discarded. Those found adequate may be reasserted with new vigor and life.

A case in point occurred at Emory University during the 1960s when T. J. Altizer was making national headlines with his death of God theology. His point of view certainly challenged traditional Christian belief. After a debate between Altizer and one of the more orthodox members of the religion faculty, a long-time Emory resident was overheard to observe that there had been more god-talk around Emory since Altizer had come on the scene than in the entire previous history of that Methodist university. Exaggerated though this claim may have been, it underlined the fact that Altizer, in challenging traditional dogma, was stimulating people to think seriously about their fundamental beliefs and commitments.

Fundamental beliefs need to be continually challenged if they are to remain alive and vigorous. Creative doubt accomplishes this. Indeed, without creative doubt how do a person's beliefs mature? Without creative doubt how does a person make his own that which he has simply inherited? It is often painful to evaluate critically one's inherited beliefs, but the pain gives birth to beliefs that are alive. Out of the pain come vital ideas that the person has made his own.

A college student encountered a professor who stimulated her to think in exciting ways about matters she had never seriously considered. Upon returning home, she began discussing with a member of her family some of the questions she was raising and some of the issues she was trying to think through. Some minutes into the conversation, she was interrupted: "If you just wouldn't think about these kinds of questions," she was admonished, "you would be so much happier." In one sense, perhaps. But also she would have been a little less human, and her fundamental beliefs would be considerably less alive.

Challenging the Adequacy of Symbols

In the third place, most, if not all, language about God is symbolic or analogical or mythological. Indeed, religious language is perhaps the language of myth and symbols *par excellence.* One is reminded again of Tillich's claim that "man's ultimate concern must be expressed symbolically, because symbolic language alone is able to express the ultimate."[14] His argument is that "the true ultimate transcends the realm of finite reality infinitely. Therefore, no finite reality can express it directly and properly."[15] At best, the finite can only point to the infinite, and symbols and myths are pointers pointing beyond themselves. Finite man labors to understand the infinite, and as he attempts to express his limited understanding, he produces a language that more or less adequately reflects the infinite.

If one grants that religious language never perfectly reflects the ultimate, is one not obliged to acknowledge this openly? Is one not obligated to doubt the full adequacy of the symbols and myths employed? And should not this doubt motivate one to work at developing language that more adequately reflects the nature of God?

Suggestive at this point is an observation made by John Stuart Mill. Honesty necessitates the recognition that if one had been born elsewhere, one would probably have adopted the religious tradition of that particular culture, whether that be Buddhism, Hinduism, Islam, or whatever.[16] Serious reflection on this fact should give rise to a kind of toleration that acknowledges that most religions seek to reflect ultimate value. Then the question becomes which religion (which set of symbols and myths) reflects ultimate value most adequately. Creative doubt encourages this question. Dogmatism and intolerance suppress this crucial inquiry.

Assume that one concludes that the symbols and myths of the Christian faith most adequately reflect ultimate value. Then the question becomes, which Christian symbols? Which myths? There is considerable diversity and disagreement even within Christendom itself. Even when one decides on a particular set of symbols, the task is not complete. For recall, no symbols are ever fully adequate to reflect the infinite. Creative doubt encourages the continual reappraisal of symbols so that they may, if possible, be replaced by more adequate reflections of the infinite.

For those who take religion seriously, at stake here is nothing less than idolatry: the one who never doubts the adequacy of his symbols is worshiping his symbols. To worship symbols is to worship the pointers to God rather than God; and to worship something other than God is, by definition, idolatry. Creative doubt, then, may serve as a check against idolatry itself.

Challenging the Quest for Certainty

Finally, consider a defense of creative doubt that involves challenging the value of the quest for certainty.

The quest for certainty (and the avoidance of doubt) often manifests itself in the effort to find some authority to whom burdensome freedom and responsibility can be surrendered. The easiest way to secure certainty is to surrender one's personal freedom and responsibility for making choices. Or, perhaps more accurately, the easiest way to secure the *illusion* of certainty is to surrender one's personal freedom and responsibility for making decisions. That this is so is the crucial point Fyodor Dostoevsky makes in "The Grand Inquisitor" passage of the *Brothers Karamazov*.[17]

Within the novel, "The Grand Inquisitor" is a story told by one brother, Ivan, to another, Alyosha. The story is set in Seville, Spain, during the period of the Inquisition. Specifically, the account relates a conversation that was to have transpired between the Grand Inquisitor, who had been in charge of burning the heretics, and Christ, who had returned momentarily to comfort the suffering.

As the confrontation develops, the Inquisitor accuses Christ of giving to man an unbearable burden—freedom. Nothing, argues the Inquisitor, has been more insupportable for human society than freedom. Did you forget that men prefer peace and even death to freedom of thought? Yet you have weighed men down with the fearful responsibility of having to choose freely the fundamental principles by which he lives. And man, who has wrestled fifteen centuries with the freedom he did not want, has finally found someone to whom he can hand over his burden; he has found an escape. Man has gratefully laid his freedom at our feet (the feet of the medieval Church). Because we, the Church, are willing to assume responsibility for the very freedom that man cannot stand, he bows before us as if we were gods. And so the Inquisitor concludes: "We have corrected Thy work and have founded it upon *miracle, mystery and authority.* And men rejoiced that they were again led like sheep, and that the terrible gift [freedom] that had brought them each suffering, was, at last, lifted from their hearts."[18]

Dostoevsky's insight is to the point. Freedom is a burden, for with freedom comes the responsibility of continually reevaluating the very foundations of one's life. This is a responsibility from which many try to escape. To flee from this burden, however, is to flee from the very freedom that is a defining characteristic of the fully human. One may quest for certainty and flee from freedom, doubt, and insecurity; but as Peter Bertocci put it, such flight "is to miss the whole point of being human."[19]

In summary, four arguments have been advanced in defense of creative doubt: (1) that such doubt is a means of constructively acknowledging human finitude, (2) that such doubt can play a crucial role in keeping one's fundamental beliefs alive and vital, (3) that, in the religious arena, such doubt is a valuable weapon against idolatry itself, and (4) that the avoidance of doubt may reflect a relinquishing of freedom and a dehumanizing quest for certainty.

A final but crucial note: Simply because there is an element of doubt and uncertainty surrounding fundamental principles should not prohibit commitment in depth to one's basic beliefs. The last thing to be encouraged is an intimidated individual, wholly indecisive and uncommitted. There is nothing incompatible between deep commitment to a principle and an open attitude (spawned by creative doubt) that makes possible a future reevaluation of that principle. There is nothing incompatible between commitment so significant that it results in action and creative doubt that challenges the individual to be open to the future and to change. It was Bertrand Russell who maintained that "to teach how to live without certainty, and yet without being paralyzed by hesitation, is perhaps the chief thing that philosophy, in our age, can still do for those who study it."[20]

Indeed, there is something majestic and compelling about the fact that in those areas of life where value is at stake, one must make an uncertain judgment and then act courageously. As someone has noted, the very essence of human dignity is the courage to be unsure.

Philip Blair Rice quotes Justice Oliver Wendell Holmes as once observing that, "'the highest courage is to stake everything on a premise that you know tomorrow may disprove.'"[21] Rice then adds an even deeper insight: "If there is a still higher courage, it stems from the realization that the premises are such that tomorrow can neither prove nor disprove them in a way that will fully still our uncertainties."[22]

Finally, as Paul Tillich puts it:

Doubt is overcome...by courage. Courage does not deny that there is doubt, but it takes the doubt into itself as an expression of its own finitude....Courage does not need the safety of an unquestionable conviction. It includes the risk without which no creative life is possible.[23]

---

1. M. de Unamuno, "Saint Emmanuel the Good, Martyr." in F. Karl and L. Hamalian, eds., *The Existential Imagination* (Greenwich: Fawcett Publications, 1963), 99.
2. Ibid., 101.
3. Ibid., 102-103.
4. Ibid., 115.
5. Ibid., 119.
6. C. S. Peirce, "Fallibilism, Continuity, and Evolution" in Hartshorne and Weiss, eds., *Collected Papers of Charles Sanders Peirce,* Volume I, *Principles of Philosophy* (Cambridge: Harvard University Press, 1960), 58-72.

7. Ibid., 60.
8. Ibid., 70.
9. P. Tillich, *Dynamics of Faith* (New York: Harper and Brothers, 1957), 1.
10. Ibid., 7.
11. Ibid., 21.
12. Ibid., 19.
13. J. Bronowski, *The Ascent of Man* (Boston: Little, Brown and Company, 1973), 374.
14. Tillich, *Dynamics of Faith,* 41.
15. Ibid., 44.
16. J. S. Mill, *On Liberty* (New York: The Liberal Arts Press, 1956), 22-23.
17. F. Dostoevsky, *The Brothers Karamazov,* trans. C. Garnett (New York: The Modern Library, 1950), 292-314.
18. Ibid., 305.
19. P. A. Bertocci, *Religion as Creative Insecurity* (New York: Association Press, 1958), IX.
20. B. Russell, *A History of Western Philosophy* (New York: Simon and Schuster, 1945), XIV.
21. P. B. Rice, *On the Knowledge of Good and Evil* (New York: Random House, 1955), 288.
22. Ibid.
23. Tillich, *Dynamics of Faith,* 101.

I have used Baird's article for two reasons. First, it says much of what I wish to say about faith and doubt, and says it very well. Second, his opening discussion of the ethics of teaching these ideas is stimulating and challenging. As one who often struggles with this problem, I find that while I often act in the manner he suggests, I am not entirely comfortable with his conclusion. I agree that one should consider questions of timing, tact, and situation before pushing such a discussion on people. Yet I am sure Baird would agree that it is dangerous and unfair to leap to assumptions about differences between college students and "simple, uneducated people" and "ninety-five-year-old grandmothers." When I teach college students they are sure that their narrow-minded parents could never deal with new ideas as openly as they. But when I teach older people, they are likely to think their children are the ones who lack the maturing for such soul searching.

There probably are individuals emotionally and intellectually unable to struggle with challenges to their fundamental beliefs and commitments, but we should be careful about stereotyping groups of people on the basis of education or cultural situation.

Beyond that problem, however, I wish to expand on one of Baird's underlying themes, as expressed in his final quotation from Paul Tillich: "Courage does not deny that there is doubt, but it takes the doubt into itself." Doubt is not the opposite of faith; it is an essential element within faith. When we are truly committed, it is precisely that commitment which should drive us to doubt the adequacy of our existing knowledge in the hope of finding an ever better understanding of the nature of that to which we are committed so that our commitment can be expressed more effectively and creatively.

It must be admitted, however, that doubt is often experienced as a threat to faith. Faith is, after all, something which arises in some context of beliefs. Many times a change of beliefs does properly lead to a change of commitments. If we find that a person we have trusted with our faith is in fact deceiving us, we will probably abandon that trust.

It would probably be helpful to expand a little on a distinction, suggested very briefly in chapter 2, between relative and absolute threats to faith. Doubt is experienced as a relative threat to our faith when it deals with particular beliefs and forces us to refine our faith but not to abandon it. Doubt is experienced as an absolute threat to faith when it is doubt about the basic worthiness of the focus of faith itself.

The prophet Jeremiah, whose words became the title for this study, may provide a helpful example. Jeremiah was a prophet of justice. He believed in a God of justice, but he did not naïvely believe that God ensured justice in every event. Instead, it was precisely his profound commitment to God and God's justice which made him so acutely aware of the injustice in the world about him. For such a sensitive person the commitment to justice in the midst of injustice is a painful experience. Hence Jeremiah is often called the "suffering prophet."

Although the reality of God seems never to have been a question for Jeremiah, he did come to seriously doubt the justice of God. God had commissioned him to call the people to act justly, or else God would justly punish them. It seemed, however, that God never backed up the message Jeremiah delivered. God not only failed to punish injustice, God seemed actually to reward it. So Jeremiah challenged God:

You have right on your side, Yahweh,
when I complain about you.
But I would like to debate a point of justice with you.
Why is it that the wicked live so prosperously?
Why do scoundrels enjoy peace?
You plant them, they take root,
and flourish, and even bear fruit.
You are always on their lips,
yet so far from their hearts.—Jeremiah 12:1, 2 JB

It seems obvious that Jeremiah dealt constantly with this relative threat to his faith. If he did not accurately understand how God meant to impose justice, how could he proclaim God's intentions? How could he continue to preach when his expectations were so different from the actual situation?

At some point or points, this relative challenge to his faith, this sense of not knowing what was going on, must have moved beyond mere frustration into challenging his fundamental commitment to the justice of God. Perhaps God was not just at all! Perhaps God was merely mocking him! It must surely have been in such a moment of struggling with this absolute threat to his most basic faith itself that he cried out,

You have seduced me, Yahweh, and I have let myself be seduced;
you have overpowered me: you were the stronger.
I am a daily laughingstock,
everybody's butt.
Each time I speak the word, I have to howl

and proclaim: "Violence and ruin!"
The word of Yahweh has meant for me
insult, derision, all day long.—Jeremiah 20:7, 8 JB

But even in this moment, Jeremiah found that his faith was too deeply a part of him to escape. Whether for good or ill, whether wisely or foolishly, he could not escape the call to proclaim justice.

I used to say, "I will not think about him,
I will not speak in his name any more."
Then there seemed to be a fire burning in my heart,
imprisoned in my bones.
The effort to restrain it wearied me,
I could not bear it.—Jeremiah 20:9 JB

Jeremiah's writings do not indicate that he ever escaped from these doubts entirely. How could he? How could any prophet of justice live out that commitment without doubts when surrounded by a world in which injustice seems so often to have the final, horrible word? To deny the reality and power of injustice or to pretend that God was obviously making it all come out for the best would have been to deny his ultimate faith commitment to opposing that injustice. The power of his preaching and prophetic writing lies largely in the very struggle he endured. It is here that we confront the depth of his passion for justice.

To Jeremiah, the question of whether God was just must have seemed like the ultimate threat to his faith. Yet from a different point of view, there may be an even more ultimate question: "Is justice itself worthy of our commitment?" Jeremiah probably could not have separated these two questions, but others have. Suppose that God is not just, or that there is no God. What does the prophet of justice do then? Is justice worthy of our commitment even if there is no ultimate justice guaranteed by a divine being?

Many people over the centuries have argued that our commitment to justice need not depend on belief in a divine judge who ensures that justice will prevail. For them, the absolute threat to faith is not any question of factual belief about the existence or character of God, but the question of faith in justice itself. Only when one asks deep in one's heart, "Is it worth the price to work for justice?" is one facing the doubt which constitutes the absolute threat to faith. Without either assuming or denying the existence of God, this latter approach is most consistent with the approach to faith taken in this book. For many Christians, the deepest, most terrifying doubt may seem to be about the existence of a divine being. But perhaps this is not the ultimate doubt. It may only be a relative threat to our most basic commitments.

Perhaps the primary question here is one of courage and integrity. We must have the courage to live with integrity whatever the outcome of our questions about God. There must be a passion for Truth in spite of finitude's necessary limitation to ambiguous, particular, and partial truths. There must be a passion for justice, for the grace of love, and for meaning in human existence. But this passion in itself must not be mistaken for evidence that there is some ultimate Justice, Love, or Meaning. The question of what we want the Truth to be and the question of what the Truth is, must not be confused. Our integrity demands that we pursue both questions in their proper ways.

If there is indeed an ultimate Justice, then we must strive with all the passion of our beings to know its nature and to answer its demands for justice. We must also have the courage to be just in spite of the fact that there may be no Justice. Likewise, if there is some inexhaustible well of gracious Love from which we may drink and be renewed for acts of love, then we must not rest until we find it. We must also have the courage to love in spite of the fact that there may be no such well. Finally, if there is a purpose of such majesty, a vision of such beauty that seeing it will transform acts of suffering, sacrifice, and drudgery into occasions of joy, then we must know this final Meaning. Yet if the world is only an accident of cold, uncaring matter, we must still have the courage to affirm the truth that we really do experience, here and now, a sense of meaningfulness in the momentary joy of love and justice. We must have a passion which drives us to seek the infinite resources we need in the face of the awful infinity of need and suffering. We must also have the integrity and courage to be creative of love and justice with the insufficient resources at hand, for they may well be all the resources there are. This last possibility, with which many modern Christians live, is well expressed in Archibald MacLeish's play, *J.B.:* "He does not love. He Is. But we do. That's the wonder."[1]

It is also helpful to distinguish between relative and absolute levels of faith. In whichever way we may identify that to which we are ultimately committed, it is important to distinguish between the final reality of that object of faith and our present understanding of it. Because of our finitude and the sinfulness which so pervades our thinking, we must constantly recognize that our present idea of God or justice or love does not fully and finally capture that ultimate reality. Perhaps the broadest way to say this is to emphasize that the truths presently within our grasp never totally express the full truth. To be ultimately committed to truth is to refuse either to settle for the partial truth which we presently have, or to blindly and dogmatically insist that our present perception of truth contains no errors.

Yet we must not let our open-mindedness prevent us from having or acting on commitments. We must never say that because we cannot know everything we can know nothing, or that because of our falibility it is not worth inquiring. We must never say that because we may not understand the full nature of justice we should not work for justice in the world.

Commitment to honesty must not destroy other commitments, but must serve them.

The tension between commitment and openness can be creative rather than paralyzing if we recognize the two-level nature of faith. At one level we must be committed to the best truth we have, to the best understanding we have of God, justice, and love. We must be prepared to act boldly and decisively on the best wisdom available to us. We must also see this active commitment as being transcended by a more fundamental commitment to the reality which we do not yet see. That second level must finally take priority over the first level. If we finally discover that our old understandings and actions, however deeply felt and however openly declared, are mistaken, if we find compelling reasons to conclude that our previous views of God, justice, or love were inadequate, then out of our ultimate commitment to that greater reality we must have the courage to change. Thus doubt remains an essential, even redemptive, element within the life of faith.

Henry Nelson Wieman, a philosopher/theologian whose writings may help us to understand this two-level character of faith, suggested that this kind of faith might express itself in the following prayer.

If what I serve with all my life be not the ultimate source of greatest good, may my misdirected efforts come to nothing in such a way as to expose my error and suggest the truth. I offer my life to what does in truth make for the greatest good even though it should be different from what I think it is. If my commitment is mistaken, I give my life and all its work to be destroyed that the good which I have failed to recognize may prevail.[2]

In other words, to give our lives wholly in faith may be to lose them. It is only with such a prayer in our hearts that we can be freed to live in the tension between faith and doubt with integrity, courage, and creativity.

Faith seeks the truth which is beyond doubt, but

which can only be sought through doubt. This challenge is presented by the classic passage from the King James translation of Job 13:15, "Though he slay me, yet will I trust in him." We now know that this is actually a poor translation of the passage. It has nevertheless become a part of our tradition with which we must come to grips.

Given the KJV rendering, it was natural to think it meant that we should trust God to protect us even when the world destroys us with war, disease, and natural disaster. If so, I do not know what sense it makes to trust God.

Yet there is a way for us to trust in God. Trusting in God means trusting in the ultimate value or sacredness of truth. This we can trust, even if it slays us.

We can and must trust in the truth because there is nowhere else we can turn, nothing else to trust. Can we trust in lies in order to avoid the painful truth? Can we trust our fantasies, our wishful beliefs, our self-deceptions, in order to hide from the way things really are? Can we trust appearance in order to escape reality? No! Even if the truth destroys our most beloved, self-serving lies, we can do no other than to trust the truth. Even if the facts disclose to us the folly of our fondest beliefs, we must embrace the facts. In short, even if reality slays the God we now see by destroying our existing ideas about God, we must trust that greater, unknown, divine truth, for there is no one and nothing else to trust. There is only truth, reality.

To trust in the Truth means to be willing to send our roots down into the darkness where we cannot yet see, to confront the unknown, and to face the pain of our own ignorance. To trust in the Truth means to be willing to send our branches skyward, leaving the security of familiar truths behind, opening ourselves to new light and new risks. To trust in the Truth means to commit ourselves to growth, to learning, to risk.

The final paradox is that trusting in God means recognizing that we must ultimately take responsibility for our own search for the Truth. Answers do not fall out of heaven undistorted by the human condition. Revelation is not God giving us infallible information. Revelation is our human encounter with that Divine Reality which is always more than we can grasp or express.

We must therefore finally take responsibility for weighing the evidence in the light of reason and for deciding what we think best expresses or points toward the Truth. Thus trusting in God means trusting also in ourselves. This may seem a paradox, but it is no contradiction. It is the root meaning of responsibility and agency.

So now the decision is before us. Will we live with faith as commitment to the Truth, or will we cling to unfounded beliefs?

Will we choose to be ultimately committed to the truth about God or to our particular beliefs about God?

Will we choose to bear the pain of growth or to remain in the comfort of ignorance?

Will we choose to risk the unknown heights and depths, or will we tell ourselves it is sin to ask questions?

Will we choose to trust in the Reality beyond our grasp, or will we cling to human-made images of God?

Summary

Baird
1. Because an age-old conflict exists between truth and happiness, creative doubt may entail pain.
2. Creative doubt functions as an expression of the awareness that humans are finite and therefore limited with respect to knowledge. One's beliefs may be mistaken.

3. Creative doubt challenges our acquired beliefs, forcing us to continually be in the process of re-evaluating them. In this way our fundamental beliefs are kept alive.
4. Creative doubt functions as a challenge to the adequacy of the symbols we use to point to our ultimate concern. Symbols are a necessary part of God-language but are never able to fully express the ultimate. We must continually seek more adequate symbolic language. This task is encouraged by creative doubt.
5. Creative doubt challenges our attempts at certainty which may reflect desire to avoid the responsibility that accompanies the freedom of being fully human.

Mesle
1. Strong commitment and creative doubt are not incompatible. Rather, doubt is an essential element of faith.
2. Doubt is experienced as a relative threat to faith when a belief or set of beliefs comes under question.
3. Doubt is experienced as an absolute threat to faith when the value of the object of our faith comes into question.
4. We must have the courage to live with integrity whatever the outcome of our factual questions about God, truth, justice, love, and meaning.
5. At the relative level of faith, we must be committed to the best truth we have and be prepared to act on that truth. The relative level of faith, however, is transcended by an absolute level of faith to which belongs our fundamental commitment. The absolute level of faith consists of the ultimate reality which we are never able to fully grasp.

Study and Discussion Questions
1. According to the author's recounting of Socrates

in dialogue with Euthyphro, when is one morally justified in holding a belief?
2. What is more important, the truth (arrived at through creative doubt) or happiness (experienced in spite of conflicting beliefs)? What does Baird suggest as a way to resolve these apparently conflicting goals?
3. How does Baird discuss the way in which creative doubt can acknowledge human limitations? Do you agree or disagree with his argument? Why?
4. In what ways can creative doubt help to keep fundamental beliefs alive? Why is it important for you to challenge your most fundamental beliefs—those which are most important to you? How does this suggestion differ from your customary method of handling and holding your strongest beliefs?
5. Why does Baird recommend that symbols contained in religious language be openly questioned and doubted? Do you agree or disagree? Why?
6. Baird makes a case for creative doubting of fundamental principles while still maintaining deep commitment to beliefs. In what ways do you agree or disagree with his argument? Why?
7. With which point offered by Baird is the author uncomfortable? What does Mesle say about this? Do you agree with Baird or Mesle? Why?
8. How does the author distinguish between relative and absolute threats to faith?
9. Is it possible within the framework of this study and the author's understanding of the relationship between faith and belief, to doubt certain attributes of God (like justice), while maintaining the *reality* of God? Why or why not? How does Jeremiah's experience clarify this relationship?
10. Why is it impossible to completely escape doubts? Why is it important not to try to escape

them? Why is it also important to welcome doubts?
11. Why must people "have the courage to live with integrity whatever the outcome of our questions about God"?
12. What value is there in affirming particular (finite) truths even when you may not know (or understand) ultimate truth completely?
13. Read again Henry Nelson Wieman's prayer. Could you offer it as your own? If so, why? If not, what prayer would you offer in contrast?
14. Identify a new insight you have gained based on your study of this chapter.

_____

_____

_____

---

1. Archibald MacLeish, J.B. (Boston: Houghton Mifflin, Co., 1958), 152.
2. Henry Nelson Wieman, "Commitment for Theological Inquiry." The Journal of Religion 42, no. 3, July, 1962, 179, 80.

Chapter 17
TWO TYPES OF THEOLOGY
PART I—AN ALLEGORY

Many readers may now be thinking: What you have said is all well and good up to a point. It is certainly true that most people believe in God without living in total commitment to God. But isn't that just a result of human weakness? Does it really have anything to do with a difference between faith and belief? After all, what sense would it make to say that someone had faith in God without believing that God exists?

Certainly human nature accounts for many of our failures to live out our commitments more fully. But this does not adequately account for the distinction that has been observed. There is still a basic difference between intellectual assent and personal commitment. The last question above is, however, important for one's approach to faith. Most readers will ask, "If it doesn't apply to the issue of faith in God, why bother?"

Perhaps the clearest way to make the distinction between faith and belief with regard to God is to examine two very different ways of doing theology. One of these forms of theology may seem very strange and puzzling to many readers. In an effort to overcome this difficulty, a small allegory about faith and belief is presented.

Imagine a mountain lake, cool as wet grass on a spring morning, clear as dew, and deep—so deep that even with a knife-sharp dive from a high rock your lungs would be screaming at you before you got halfway to the bottom. When the clouds are not hoarding its warmth for themselves, the sun's rays streak deeply into the lake like stage lights for an aquatic ballet performed by glittering schools of fish amid swaying, floating reeds and lily pads. A careful, patient swimmer can almost enter the dance before the local troupe feels upstaged and departs in a huff to the wings. But as one continues downward, the reach of illuminating rays is exceeded, and vision is lost in the obscurity common to all deep places. The water here is no less clear, no less vital; there is just too much of it. Mystery is always present in the depths of things.

Four people live in the forest surrounding the lake. Their feelings and ideas about the lake vary greatly.

Eric and Erin believe the lake is inhabited by a water spirit. They believe that the spirit holds the power of life and death over all who enter the water. The spirit has established laws. Those who believe and obey the laws will be supported by the spirit and may swim safely. Those who do not know or do not obey the laws will flounder in the depths.

Eric worships the water and the spirit. As the home of the spirit, the lake is a sacred place for Eric. When he enters the water, he obeys the law of the lake strictly. In return he feels the water support him, embrace him, comfort and soothe him. He feels communion with the spirit of the lake, especially when diving into its depths. For Eric, the lake is the center of life.

Erin believes that there is a spirit, but fears it. She is not a very good swimmer. She feels threatened and suffocated when she goes too far into the lake. So she stays near the edge or out of the water entirely whenever possible. She becomes angry when Eric tries to persuade her to venture farther out, or to immerse herself completely in the water. She actually wishes there were no spirit in the lake at all.

Jim and Rachel do not believe that any spirit inhabits the lake. Both know the basic chemistry of water, the physical laws of buoyancy, the mechanics of swimming, and the hazards of cramps and currents without believing them to be the laws or actions of a supernatural being or spirit. But Jim and Rachel feel as differently about the lake as do Eric and Erin.

Jim hates the lake. A good friend of his drowned there. Jim tends to view the lake as a monster waiting to suck innocent people into its depths. The water seems frigid and threatening. He prefers to drink from smaller pools of water in the mountains and avoid the lake altogether.

Rachel is enthralled by the beauty and vitality of the lake. She loves to escape the world of gravity and to move in the three-dimensional world of water as a bird flies in the world of air. She can splash and frolic with the lake as her playmate or experience quiet communion by sinking into its depths. Rachel has respect and reverence for the lake and a sense of joy whenever she enters it. For Rachel, the lake is the center and giver of life.

Although Eric and Rachel are worlds apart in their ideas about the lake, they share a common communion with it. It has grasped both of them and become the center around which their lives revolve.

We can imagine different ways in which they might react to each other.

It might be that Eric views Rachel primarily as an unbeliever who denies the existence of a water spirit. If that is the central feature of Eric's understanding of Rachel, he will obviously be suspicious of her, and perhaps unfriendly. At the same time, Rachel may see Eric as a naïve, rather unsophisticated person who operates out of superstitions.

It may be however, that Eric and Rachel are able to see past their differences of belief and recognize their common faith in the lake. They may sense their shared respect and reverence for the water of the lake as the "giver of life" and they may be able to join at times in their communion with the lake. If Eric has songs or poems extolling the greatness and love of the water spirit, Rachel may even be able to sing and recite these with him, viewing them as symbolic poetry which expresses her own feelings of reverence and joy as well as Eric's.

If they are able to understand each other in this way, they will probably be able to work together in caring for the lake. They can cooperate in keeping the lake free of litter and in fighting against pollution. They can stand together in defense of the lake.

At points, though, they may come into conflict because their common faith is still rooted in vastly different beliefs. Eric may have certain ritual rules about how or when one may enter the lake. He may limit or forbid catching fish in the lake on the grounds that they are the property of the spirit. Rachel may see these rules as violations of her legitimate rights to use the lake in her own manner and to catch fish for food. Some of these conflicts can be resolved through mutual respect and open communication. Others will remain problems.

Eric may have difficulty understanding Rachel's lack of belief in the water spirit, especially if they are aware of their common faith. "How can you experience the ecstasy of commuion with the lake and not believe in the spirit with whom you commune?" he might ask her. "How can you be so hypocritical as to use the laws of the spirit without acknowledging that they come from an intelligent ruler of the lake? How can you feel the loving embrace of the water and not believe in the one who embraces you?"

In response, Rachel may ask how Eric can possibly believe—or need to believe—in such a spirit. "Chemistry and physics account very adequately for the laws of the lake. No spirit is needed to explain floating and sinking." Further, Rachel may say, "Why must I take the symbols of your songs and poems literally? The water gives life; hence I respect and revere it. The lake gives me joy and freedom; hence I celebrate it. The lake gives me peace and comfort; hence I love it. Why do you need to create some spirit in order to enjoy these things?"

In our imagination, we can think of Eric and Rachel working together during the day to care for the lake and swimming together in its coolness. In the evening we can imagine them eating supper together by the lake and discussing their different beliefs about it, probing each other's ideas, challenging each other's thinking, sharing each other's experiences. As night comes, they may join together in a song or poem in honor of the lake, enjoying and declaring their common faith.

PART II—INTERPRETATION OF THE ALLEGORY

The interpretation of this allegory should be fairly obvious in most respects. The lake represents the whole world—the universe in which we live. There are two questions to be raised. First, what do you *believe* about the world? Second, how do you *feel* about the world? The characters in the allegory represent four different ways in which people may answer these two questions. They are described in a way designed to illustrate two ideas about faith and belief. First, not all people have the same beliefs and feelings about the world; there may be good reasons for their different points of view. Second, beliefs and feelings about the world do not always go together in the same way for all people. People who share common beliefs may feel very differently about life; while people with very different beliefs may share common concerns and commitments.

There is another reason for the allegory being constructed in this way. For most people it is very difficult to understand radically different points of view. Specifically, it is hard for Christians who hold traditional beliefs about God to understand how or why someone might hold a different view, or how someone who does not share their view of God might still have a very similar faith and even be able to use religious language. The allegory may help some readers make this leap of understanding.

There is one potential difficulty which should receive comment. Traditional Christian belief in God is not intended to be seen just like a primitive belief that lakes are inhabited by spirits. Obviously this is not the case. It is done only to put the question in a different light in order to accomplish the purposes described above.

Both within and outside of church communities, there exist people with feelings and beliefs like those of Eric, Erin, Jim, and Rachel as well as a variety of other points of view. Some have often wondered how it was that people with very strong fundamentalist beliefs could have no church affiliations at all, while others actively participating in a church indicate they long ago stopped believing that any divine being rules the world. Obviously, many people who stop believing in the existence of God tend to lose the religious faith that was tied to those beliefs. But others have retained a strong commitment to people, the world, and even to their religious communities. The symbols of God's love—the crucified Christ and continuing revelation, for example—have remained for them as powerful expressions of their deepest concerns and commitments. These symbols have pointed to something which has grasped them, even while their beliefs have undergone radical changes.

While it is important for us to understand people whose perspectives are like those of Erin and Jim in the allegory, and while we realize that there are many other perspectives as well, attention will be focused here on the figures of Eric and Rachel—those who have a positive faith despite contrasting beliefs.

Eric and Rachel

Eric and Rachel have a common faith. They have similar feelings about the lake. Both feel respect, reverence, and even love for the lake. Both are grasped by the water as the source of life and the lake as the center of their lives. Both are committed to caring for the lake. Yet their faiths are interwoven with quite different sets of beliefs.

This relationship between faith and belief is also present in the diversity of Christianity. Many Christians share a common faith while holding very different beliefs. The purpose of this chapter is to describe two such approaches to Christian faith. The first will be a common form of theology with which most readers can readily identify. It is one which attempts to speak literally, as far as possible, about a supreme being—God. The second approach is one in which language about God is seen as a set of poetic symbols expressing a way of being grasped by an ultimate commitment to and reverence for the world and human existence. This approach is one which may seem strange to many readers, but which has in fact spoken very powerfully to many Christians. In both cases, the question of belief in relation to faith will be addressed.

Presuppositions: Christian Experience

Just as Eric and Rachel shared a common sense of communion with the lake, many Christians share a common sense of encounter with divine grace. Of course, most traditional religious expression commonly arises by childhood training rather than by conversation and independent reflection. Yet it comes alive more powerfully when it starts fresh from personal reflection on the experience of being grasped by an encounter with the divine. Probably no two people experience this ultimate reality in exactly the same way. For purposes of this discussion, however, I will suggest some elements which are very common in Christian religious experience.

Some of these common elements of the Christian experience of faith are

>   the sense of encounter;
>   the sense of being unconditionally and overwhelmingly loved;
>   the sense that this love affirms the ultimate worth and dignity of persons, perhaps of the whole world, and even of "Being" itself;
>   the sense that life can be meaningful;
>   the sense that the sacredness which has been encountered in one place and in one moment may be encountered in all places and in all events if we are open to it;
>   the sense that the love we have encountered calls us into responsible love for others in the world.

These elements have intentionally been expressed as descriptions of experience rather than as affirmative statements about God. In the allegory, Eric and Rachel shared similar experiences but interpreted them differently. The same is true here. The two kinds of theology are two ways in which people may convert these experiences into affirmations, that is, beliefs. Readers should remember, however, that there are many other ways in which religious people have experienced and conceived of reality.

Traditional Theism (Eric)

Eric's belief in the spirit of the lake represents what is probably the most common form of traditional Christian belief about God. God exists as a spirit who rules the universe. Eric represents the person who believes in God as a personal being.

In traditional theism, God is personal, even though infinite and eternal. Within this general framework, the elements of Christian experience described above may be translated into a set of affirmations something like this:

> I encountered a person, God. God loves me unconditionally and overwhelmingly. This sense of being loved filled me with a sense of my own worth and dignity in the sight of God. I realized that God's love and power fill the whole world. The world is God's, along with all the people in it. God loves the world and its people. God is omnipotent (all powerful), omnipresent (everywhere present), and omniscient (all knowing). This experience with God has given my life a new sense of meaning. I am living in God's world and am called to do God's work. God's love calls me to go into the world and rejoice in loving service to others.

If we asked Eric why he believes in God's existence, the answer would be obvious and immediate. "I have encountered God. I have felt God's love for me. How could I doubt the existence of God?" Given such a powerful experience, and such certainty of belief, it is difficult to distinguish between faith and belief. The experience of being grasped is identical with the evidence for belief. The encounter which creates faith also affirms belief. Does this distinction have any real meaning here? Before attempting to answer that question, the point of view represented by Rachel will be described.

An Alternative Theology (Rachel)

In the allegory, Rachel represents a point of view which has deep roots in Christian history, and which has been very influential in this century. It is harder to define than the traditional form of theism, but it bascially involves feeling about the world as Rachel feels about the lake. Such a person might explain a religious experience with the same elements given above in terms something like the following:

> I have had a powerful experience of the sacredness of the world. Although I do not believe in any supernatural or supreme being, I sometimes use the word "God" to name what I experienced. "God," for me, is the symbolic or poetic name for that sacredness which I encountered. I feel that the world really matters, that it is ultimately significant. Persons have infinite worth and dignity, simply because they are persons and part of the world. To feel sacredness and worth is like feeling loved, unconditionally. In fact, I sometimes use the symbolic language, "God loves us" to express how I feel.
>
> It is obvious to me that the sacredness or holiness I experienced is something which applies to the whole world. This is like saying that God is everywhere (omnipresent). In the same way, every event has the potential for revealing this sacredness. That is the meaning for me of God's omnipotence—not that God is a powerful being, but that every event reveals a creative sacredness in the world. Everything I do makes a difference to the world and to my life. That is what I mean when I talk about God knowing and caring about everything that happens.
>
> It is impossible for me to experience this tremendous sense of the worth and sacredness of the world and of people without feeling involved in and responsible for the world. If all people have infinite worth, how can I stand by and see people die of hunger or in war? Their lives are sacred. The same is true of the environment and the animals. The world is holy. I cannot shirk my calling to care for it. I am in love with the world. I rejoice in its beauty and wonder. I commune with it and play in it. I have felt its holiness.

Rachel does not believe in the existence of a God who rules the world or loves it, but she is nevertheless grasped by a sense of the world's sacredness. For her, natural explanations are adequate for questions about how the world works. Especially when speaking to her more traditional friends, however, her sense of awe about the world sometimes leads her to use religious language to express her feelings. She can speak poetically about her experience of sacredness by saying that she has felt God's love for herself and the world.

Faith and Belief

Just as in the allegory, Eric and Rachel share a common sense of commitment, concern, and even love, yet their beliefs are quite different. Their religious experiences may have been similar, but their interpretations of those experiences are different. Eric experienced the love of a personal divine being while Rachel experienced a sense of the sacredness of the world and of her life. From that basic difference, their theologies go in different directions. Yet they continue to share a similar faith—a similar sense of being grasped, concerned, and committed—even a similar sense of being loved so much that they are moved to love those about them. Rachel can even feel comfortable at times using traditional Christian language as either poetic or symbolic ways of expressing her faith.

As strange as Rachel's religion may seem to some readers, it is not uncommon in the history of Christianity. Mystics have often described their views in these terms. In the eighteenth and nineteenth centuries many educated people turned to similar views, partly as a result of growing scientific knowledge. In the twentieth century the horrors of the wars and the concentration camps have also driven large numbers of Christians and Jews away from their traditional belief in a divine being who rules the world. For many, however, their Christian faith in the worth and dignity of persons and of the world has not been lost with these beliefs. Often, it has been translated into terms very similar to Rachel's. Faith has essentially remained, while beliefs have been radically altered or even abandoned.

Eric and Rachel Together

How can people like Eric and Rachel relate to each other? Just as in the allegory, there are many possibilities. All too often differences of belief become the focal point rather than the common faith. Sometimes people like Eric tend to be suspicious of people like Rachel. And people like Rachel may sometimes fail to appreciate the beliefs of people like Eric. The result is that people divide into camps of "believers" and "unbelievers" in a way which obscures their common commitments and concerns.

As already indicated in the allegory, it would be more productive if the Erics and Rachels of the world would stress their common faith so they can work together to care for the world and its people. There are urgent needs which can only be met by the cooperation of all those who are deeply concerned and committed. Beyond the immediate work which demands this cooperation, there is surely much which could be learned in dialogue between such people. The opportunity for expanded communion is itself worth seeking.

Faith and Belief for Eric

Our immediate concern, however, is not with these problems but with the struggle to understand the nature of Christian faith. Having examined Rachel's theology, we now can deal with the question posed at the conclusion of the section on Eric. How are faith and belief to be distinguished for Eric?

It has already been stressed that the experience of love which created Eric's faith in God is also the reason for his firm belief in God's existence. In such cases the distinction between faith and belief blurs as the two genuinely overlap. For most practical purposes Eric would probably see no real difference between his faith and belief. In his own mind it is precisely his belief in God by which he is grasped. His belief enables him to enter into communion with

God and to know God. It would be impossible for Eric to explain or talk about his faith without talking about his beliefs. For him they are virtually one and the same. Eric could not conceive of experiencing God's love without believing in the existence of God.

The reason we must qualify this identity between faith and belief for Eric, as a matter of Eric's perspective, is that there are people who share Eric's beliefs without having his powerful faith. These people hold belief in God only as an intellectual assent. They are not grasped by it as Eric is. They are not ultimately concerned about and committed to God as Eric is. They believe *without* faith.

It is also clear that Eric's faith in God is not merely a matter of belief without evidence. Many of his specific notions about God may not rest on direct evidence; but with regard to his sense of knowing a loving God, his whole life is the evidence. His encounter with the love of God permeates his life so that he can hardly question its reality. That experience of love is both the evidence for his beliefs and the foundation of his faith.

Faith and Belief for Rachel

Obviously, Rachel's faith is not identical with Eric's. She is not grasped by a belief that God exists. But she is grasped by something. By what is she grasped? Different people in Rachel's situation may answer that question very differently, for that "something" is very difficult to express. She may use words like *sacred, holy,* and *worth* to describe her feelings. She may, at times, even use language similar to Eric's, though not necessarily. But Rachel does not explain her experience by referring to beliefs about a divine being.

Rachel may or may not try to explain her sense of sacredness by referring to her beliefs about the world. Some people experience the sacred almost completely apart from any rational account of the nature of the universe. Physical laws may not hold that dynamic power to grasp them. Others, often scientists, are powerfully grasped by the scientific vision of the vastness and complexity of the world: the sense that we are part of a cosmic evolutionary process, that our bodies are made of matter forged in the heart of distant stars, and that the human race may someday voyage amidst those stars—may all be elements for some Rachels in their experience of the sacred. As always, we cannot make rigid rules about how her faith and belief shall be related.

Reality, Faith, and Life

Using Christian language, we can say that Eric and Rachel are both grasped by "God." They have encountered something sacred, but they understand that encounter differently. Eric experienced the encounter as meeting a personal, loving being. Rachel experienced the encounter as a disclosure of the sacredness of life and the world. Yet it is clear that, in many ways, they seem to be grasped by a similar faith. They have similar concerns about and commitments to the world and the people around them. Both speak of the worth of persons, of the call to love others, and of a new life of dedication.

It seems likely that while Eric and Rachel have acquired or developed their beliefs because of different experiences in their upbringing and/or education, their common faith may arise from common experiences which their beliefs interpret differently. They both see the beauty of the lake and recognize its power to give life. Both have had profound, life-shaping experiences of peace, joy, and insight in the presence of the lake. Thus, it seems very probable that their beliefs could be exchanged while their faith remained largely intact.

Faith, Belief, and Truth

The question of truth still remains. Whose idea of

reality is nearer the truth? Truth is important. The more nearly our beliefs correspond to reality, the more effective our actions are likely to be. The vast majority of Christians over the centuries—though not all—have affirmed that Eric's view is basically true. If we assume that Eric is correct, then it seems reasonable to argue that those who believe in God will be better able to share in communion with God and be led by the Holy Spirit. Thus the scriptures are far from neutral on the issue of belief in God. In the words of Hebrews 11:6, "For whoever would draw near to God must believe that he exists and that he rewards those who seek him."

Of course, Rachel would say that her view is nearer the truth than Eric's. She might argue that Eric's belief in God is simply a way of explaining the sense of the sacred which people experience. She might also suggest that belief in God or gods has often taken very destructive forms which deny human worth or lead people into wars and oppression. She would certainly point to the problem of evil, and would point out that as science expands human knowledge, Eric's God seems increasingly unnecessary to explain the world or its workings. From Rachel's perspective, God no more exists as a separate being than does the spirit in the lake.

Rachel and Eric represent only two of many responsible positions held by modern Christians. The rise of science and the massive evil seen in this century have produced renewed struggles with the problem of the truth about God. Persons deeply committed to the Christian tradition have declared such varied views as that God is not a supreme being but is Being Itself, that "God" is a primitive idea we must outgrow, and that God exists but has only persuasive power and cannot prevent evil. Others have emphasized that God is found in the lives of persons. It is vital to remember that, given the mystery of reality, we must try to respect all serious attempts to make progress toward discovery of the truth.

The issue of truth is important. Consequently, the issue of what beliefs should inform our faith will continue to be a vital one. As we have seen, however, there is also a matter of the truth of faith which is separate from the truth of belief. If Eric and Rachel can look beyond their (important) differences of belief, each may be able to affirm that there is also important truth in the other's faith. The values by which they are grasped are essentially the same in most cases. And they are both equally true to the faith they have. Their faiths also make them true to the Christian calling to love others and to care for the world over which we are stewards.

Conclusion

This exploration has taken us into ideas and perspectives which may be new for many readers. It may be helpful to once again stress that this is not a book about the nature (or even the existence) of God. It is a book about faith. And it is often helpful in trying to understand something to see it in extreme cases. That is what has been attempted here. By setting the relationship of faith and belief into an extreme contrast, the nature of that relationship has, it is hoped, been illuminated.

Summary

1. Persons who share common beliefs may feel quite differently about life, God, the church, or any other concern, while persons with quite different beliefs may share common concerns and commitments.
2. Some elements are common in Christian religious experience. The different ways in which people interpret these elements give rise to different theologies. These elements include the sense of encounter with the Divine, the sense of being unconditionally and overwhelmingly loved, an af-

firmation of the worth and dignity of all of being, the sense of the potential meaningfulness of life, the sense that the sacredness connected with the divine encounter is latent within all experience, and the sense of being called to love others.
3. Traditional theism holds that God is a personal, infinite, eternal being who rules the universe. Here the distinction between faith and belief may be especially difficult to locate. The distinction is observable in the fact that it is possible to hold beliefs without being grasped by them. Persons may believe without faith.
4. Many Christians have been and are grasped by a sense of the sacredness of the world while not accepting the outlook of traditional theism. For those persons, natural processes are adequate for explaining how the world works. These persons may use religious language to poetically express their experience of sacredness.
5. Differences in belief between persons must not be allowed to obscure a common faith.
6. A person's faith is often able to endure even the most traumatic changes in beliefs.
7. The truth of beliefs, although important, is, at least partly, a separate matter from the truth of faith.

Study and Discussion Questions
1. What is the meaning of the author's allegory?
2. In what way do Eric and Rachel—though holding different ideas about the lake—share a common communion with it? What benefits might there be in such a common communion?
3. What is your general response to the author's interpretation of the allegory?
4. On a scale of one to ten, rate how helpful or unhelpful you feel allegory is in illustrating both how and why persons may have different points

of view and beliefs stemming from common experiences.

Very Helpful				Helpful			Unhelpful		
10	9	8	7	6	5	4	3	2	1

Discuss your rating with another person or in a group.

5. Are you presently aware of others who, like you, are committed to the chruch, even though you know they hold beliefs different from yours? What has been your attitude toward these persons in the past? Has the material in this book changed, in any way, your attitude toward them? If so, how? How does it help to view your different beliefs as being only symbolic of something larger, something which neither of you can fully (or correctly) comprehend? Explain your answer.
6. Do you agree or disagree with the author's suggested common elements in the Christian experience? Why? How many of these do you hold? How may they provide enough of a common ground on which you may commune with other Christians? What more (or less) do you need?
7. Which view—Eric's traditional theism or Rachel's alternative theology—is closest to your own? Which elements are of particular importance to you? Why?
8. In what ways are you uncomfortable with a view (theology) that is farthest from your own? Do you see any reason why you could not enter into dialogue with others holding a different point of view? In what ways might it be helpful to emphasize not the particular *beliefs* but the common *experience* which gave rise to the different beliefs?
9. How has the allegory helped you to see the value of separating faith from belief?

10. What is the relationship between faith and belief for Eric? For Rachel?
11. How can people like Eric and Rachel relate to each other?
12. How might both Eric and Rachel's faith survive changing beliefs? In what ways can you apply this to your own life?
13. Why is it important to separate true faith from true belief? In your attempt to reconcile differences between yourselves and others, on which ground is your best chance for reconciliation—on true faith or true belief? How have you related to others in the past? What has been the result of efforts at reconciliation?
14. Describe your feelings resulting from a study of this chapter.

Chapter 18
FAITH, FREEDOM, AND GROWTH

If you casually ask someone what it means to be free, you will very likely be told, "Freedom means doing what I want to do." This rough definition of freedom has been crucial to much of traditional Christian theology because it is entirely compatible with predestination. If freedom is the prerequisite for moral responsibility, and if freedom is doing what we want to do, then there is no contradiction in saying that we are predestined to want to sin, and thus sin freely, making us morally responsible for what God has determined from eternity that we shall do. Under this view of freedom, it does not matter why we want to do something; we are free as long as we can do what we want to do.

This view of freedom has other important consequences. After all, people may be very largely predetermined by their heredity and by their physical and social environment. Freedom as the ability to do what we want to do is totally compatible with all forms of determinism and even with brainwashing. If you are brainwashed to want to give all your money to a cult leader, you give your money freely.

This form of freedom is powerfully illustrated in Aldous Huxley's short novel *Brave New World*. Huxley describes an imaginary utopia of the future in which everyone is happy and free. Babies are mass-produced in test tubes which run along an assembly line. Each future citizen is predestined to fill a particular spot in the social machinery. Those destined for lower class work are given lower mentalities by depriving them of oxygen for a specified period, and are given a shorter stature by having alcohol injected into their bottles. Different forms of conditioning produce different levels of intelligence. Once born, the children are subject to further conditioning. Babies are shown brightly colored books and are then shocked when they approach them, in order to assure that they will always hate books. All citizens are subjected to "sleep teaching" in which social class distinction, being happy in one's work, and the morality of the brave new world are all taught through thousands of repetitions of simple sayings, which are whispered in the children's ears every night.

On reaching adulthood, every citizen is totally conditioned to be happy in a particular class and job, to operate by a specified morality, and to hold certain beliefs unshakably. Within these predestined bounds they are entirely free. Society provides them abundantly with everything they have been taught to want: material goods, sexual satisfaction, and religious ecstasy. In the brave new world, all citizens are free to do exactly as they wish, that is, what they have been conditioned to want to do.

Obviously, most of us would find such freedom

unsatisfying. It does not really seem to be what we mean by freedom. Instead, what we mean by freedom is the ability to choose between meaningful alternatives. Certainly this includes the notion of choosing what we want to choose, but it is more. This view insists that before we can think of ourselves as truly free, we must have the power to recognize, understand, and choose among two or more significantly different possibilities. Admittedly, the idea of significance is relative to the subject. Yet the intent of this approach to freedom is to affirm that predestination, social determinism, and brainwashing are in conflict with meaningful freedom.

The failure to distinguish between these two forms of freedom may be partly responsible for the tendency of many people to identify religious freedom with the right to hold faith as beliefs without evidence. As one student wrote in an exam on this topic:

This is why America is called the "land of the free." Because we have so much freedom. This is why faith is defined as "belief without evidence," because we have the freedom to believe anything we want, without having to prove whether we're right or wrong.

In one sense this student is absolutely correct; freedom to believe purely on the basis of desire without reference to standards of truthfulness is certainly the freedom to do whatever one wants. Yet it is a very pitiful form of freedom. Even if we could walk into a shop marketing various sets of beliefs and choose the one we happened to fancy the most, this would hardly be meaningful freedom. Obviously we do not acquire our beliefs in that way. We acquire our earliest beliefs from those about us—our parents, our friends, and our society. We do not choose our earliest beliefs.

If we were to adhere rigidly to the notion that we must simply believe without question and without evidence whatever we have been taught to believe, then our beliefs would be entirely the result of chance. Like a lottery, we would win by accident of birth the beliefs of whatever community we happened to enter. Being prohibited from questioning or doubting, we could never change our beliefs. Being also taught to believe that these are the best beliefs and that we are fortunate to have them, we would certainly want to hold them. Thus we would be freely believing what we wanted to believe. But such freedom would be entirely arbitrary, nothing but chance. We would be exactly as free to choose our beliefs as we are to choose our parents.

Faith as belief without evidence is entirely compatible with the freedom to believe whatever we want to believe, or more clearly, the freedom to believe whatever we have been taught to want to believe by whoever happened to get to us first with a prepared set of beliefs. Faith as belief without evidence—without doubt, without examination—is the faith of the brave new world. It is faith without intelligence, without reason, without choice. It is faith without true freedom, the freedom to choose between meaningful alternatives.

In contrast, faith as commitment to the truth is the foundation of true freedom. We cannot and need not change the fact that we grow up with some inherited beliefs. That in itself is not bad. We need a base from which to work. Yet we must also have the ability and freedom to examine those beliefs, to doubt them, to criticize them, to compare them honestly and seriously with other beliefs, and to make genuine choices about which beliefs seem to us to most accurately tell the truth about the world. Faith as commitment to truth through growth of understanding is the foundation of such freedom.

The freedom given by such faith is the freedom to think for oneself, and like all freedoms, it is won only at a price. The price of intellectual freedom includes the willingness to give up the security of familiar, comfortable beliefs when those beliefs can no longer be justified by honest inquiry. The price of intellectual freedom also includes hard work and hard thought. Disciplined study and reflection are necessary to provide the accuracy of information, rigorous adherence to the facts, logical consistency, and clarity of statement which are inescapable prerequisites to freedom of thought.

Images of Faith to Grow

When Wallace B. Smith first explained the Presidency's Faith to Grow program for the Saints' church, he used an image which is very appropriate here. Faith, he said, is not an anchor to hold us back in safe harbors. Faith is rather the sail of our ship which catches the breath of the Spirit and moves us out into the larger, often rougher, seas. Thus faith involves risk, but it also empowers us with freedom for growth. Faith moves us beyond what we now see into areas which are yet uncharted. This is a powerful image of a faith which frees us and calls us rather than protects us, which compels us rather than restrains us, which moves us forward into the unknown rather than confining us to the known. It is a good image for a faith to grow.

Two other images of a growing faith were shared with me by Katherine Reeds during a class I taught on the nature of faith. Katherine knew something of what she spoke. Born and raised in Germany, she witnessed the devastation of World War II. Toward the end of the war she spent a brief period in a Russian prisoner-of-war camp in Czechoslovakia before a second effort at escape was successful. She walked back to Germany. Katherine remembers what it meant to be hungry and cold.

These experiences obviously had a powerful effect on her religious faith and beliefs. She had been taught as a child that God watched over every sparrow. How then could there be so much suffering by so many innocent people? Was God so busy watching sparrows that God had forgotten to care for people? Katherine still struggles with these questions, but they have forced her faith to grow. In our class, she shared two different images to express how she felt about this growth.

There are crabs which must shed their shells the way snakes shed their skins. They have to molt because their bodies must grow to live. But their shells cannot grow because they are made of dead material. If the crabs could not shed their hard shells, they would die in them. So they crawl up onto the beach, crack open their protective covers and crawl out of them. Eventually they grow new shells for protection—which in turn they will have to outgrow—but for a while they are open, exposed, unprotected against the elements and their enemies. It can be very cold and windy—very frightening—on the beach without a shell. The choice is between growth and death, so the crabs choose growth.

"This is how it was for me," Katherine told us. "My old faith could no longer fit my life—no longer make sense of my reality. I had no choice but to break it open and crawl out. It is very cold without a rigid faith to protect me; this was what I had to do, however, to grow and live."

Katherine then told us a story. When she was a little girl, she lived near a river. A large old tree had fallen into the river and was stuck a few yards off shore with a branch sticking up out of the water. Even though she could not swim very well, she loved the water, so she learned to swim just out to the tree. She could swim just that far, rest, and then swim back—no farther. One day she swam out to the tree as usual, and when she grabbed the branch it broke and sent her down into the rushing water. Having had no chance to rest, she was certain that she could not swim back to shore. As she fell, however, her feet landed suddenly on what was apparently the main trunk of the tree. This part of the tree was larger and stronger; she had never discovered it before because in order to stand on it she had to be immersed right up to her chin. It had been there all along, though she had never discovered it until her usual, weaker supports failed her.

This, she said, was how she experienced her personal growth in faith. She had not always chosen to grow. Growth had often been forced upon her in ways that were threatening and frightening. Yet when her old faith could no longer hold her up against the churning rush of life, when she had sunk deeper into life, she had found a stronger, larger faith deep down under the surface where she had not gone before.

Because our lives are different, these images may speak to us in different ways. They may not describe some persons' experience at all. Yet most of the people in that class responded with nods of assent, and I knew that while my struggles were not comparable to hers, her images told at least parts of my story, too. I had been the naked crab on a beach, and I had discovered unexpected resources of faith when up to my chin in life. Katherine's images gave rise to my own reflections on how faith might grow in relation to beliefs. While this could be expressed in many images, I found the following story helpful.

Imagine a self-indulgent woman who is looking for something to do with her life. What she needs is something worth doing, something important to make her life worth the effort. She needs to have her soul saved from nothingness.

As a test, she volunteers to work as a fund raiser for a hunger relief agency. It works! This is really worth doing! Hungry children are being fed; lives are being saved. Her worth as a person becomes centered around this mission to feed the hungry. So crucial is this organization to her self-esteem that at first she cannot tolerate hearing any criticism of it. It must be perfect or she is threatened. She could not bear the thought that her efforts might not be perfectly effective.

As she takes on more responsibility and sees more of the picture she begins to have some of her own ideas about how the agency should be run. This step involves a mild discomfort. Before she can accept the need for improvements, she must admit the imperfection of the present system. While uncomfortable, this is not traumatic because of her excitement over possibilities for growth and improvement.

Once this step is taken she is both freed and driven to begin asking questions. She examines every aspect of the part of the organization for which she is responsible. Her commitment to the organization no longer prevents her from seeing its weaknesses. Rather, her commitment is what pushes her to criticize it and work to improve it.

Our imaginings might well end here, having made the point that it is a very insecure faith which refuses to examine or doubt. But Katherine Reed's stories led me to add a further step to my own image of faith. Imagine that one day the woman discovers that the organization is not accomplishing what she thought it was. Much of the money she has raised has not gone to help hungry people; it has been lost in the bureaucracy. She is horrified. The foundations of her sense of personal worth and meaningfulness have been shattered. She feels that it has all been a self-deception to boost her ego, and she begins to sink. She quits the agency and resolves to return to her life of self-indulgence. Her dreams of changing the world are cast aside as illusions.

Soon she begins to have dreams. She dreams of hungry children whose parents must watch helplessly. She dreams of herself helping the parents to feed the children, watching them grow and learn to feed others. Her heart is filled with joy. She knows what really matters to her. After one such dream she awakens with the realization that her faith was not fundamentally in the agency itself, but in its mission, or really, in the children. The agency, though important, is not an end in itself. She is in love with hungry children who need her help, and she cannot abandon them.

We need not imagine the details of how she responds to this call. Perhaps she returns to transform the agency and set it in order as a tool for faith. She has learned about the faith of crabs and swimmers and has suffered the pains of growth. She has left her old, small shell behind, and has found a stronger, deeper foundation than she had known. That foundation lay not in specific beliefs, but in an ultimate commitment which formed the center of her life—a commitment to truth and to love.

Like Jeremiah and Amos, she hears a call which names her, and which she cannot deny.

> There seems to be a fire burning in her heart,
> imprisoned in her bones.
> The effort to restrain it wearies her,
> and she can not bear it.
>
> The Lion roars: who can help feeling afraid?
> The children call: who can refuse to help?

She has discovered the faith to be free and to grow.

Summary

1. Freedom, defined as doing what we want to do, is entirely compatible with predestination and brainwashing. As Aldous Huxley's *Brave New World* points out, one may be free to do exactly what one wants to do, but if what one wants to do is the result of predestination, brainwashing, or social conditioning, this type of freedom must be seen as meaningless and unsatisfactory.
2. What we usually mean by freedom is the ability to choose between meaningful alternatives. This meaningful freedom is in direct conflict with pre-

destination, social conditioning, and brainwashing.
3. Failure to distinguish between these two types of freedom may be partially responsible for the tendency of many people to identify religious freedom with the right to hold faith as beliefs without evidence.
4. We do not choose our earliest beliefs; we acquire them by association. Therefore, if we rigidly adhere to the claim that we should accept inherited beliefs without question and without evidence, our belief systems would be entirely the result of chance. In this situation, we are exactly as free to choose our beliefs as we are to choose our parents. Although this may be doing what one wants to do, it is not true freedom involving meaningful alternatives.
5. Faith, as commitment to truth through growth of understanding, is the foundation of true freedom. True freedom is the freedom to think for oneself and is gained at the expense of doctrinal security. It also costs hard work and hard thought.
6. Faith to grow frees us and calls us rather than protects us; it compels us rather than restrains us; and it moves us forward into the unknown rather than confining us to the known.
7. When the choice is between the growth of our faith and the death of our faith, we must choose growth.
8. Growth of faith is often forced upon us by unexpected and frightening experiences in our lives. Immersion in life may lead to deeper, stronger foundations for our faith. This foundation will consist not of beliefs, but of commitments.

Study and Discussion Questions
1. What is your definition of freedom? How does the author define it? How are they similar or different?

2. How does believing without evidence leave your beliefs purely to chance? In what ways might this type of believing correspond to a faith of "the brave new world"?
3. What is the price of intellectual freedom?
4. Which image of faith the author describes is most meaningful to you? Why? What other image may be more meaningful to you? How do these images relate to a growing faith?
5. How have your growing images of faith caused you to leave your "old shell" in search of a new one? If you have found a new shell, what is it? How is this new shell so comfortable that you might not want to outgrow it? How is this a problem?
6. Which feeling do you now think is most important to cultivate—security in current beliefs about God, faith, and life, or commitment to truth and love? Why?
7. What is the nature of the fire burning in your heart, imprisoned in your bones? Share your faith statement with another person. Why is this the kind of fire you never want to put out? How can you keep it going? How willing are you to give yourself to this effort as a lifelong commitment? Why?
8. What is your faith like today? Share with another person where you are currently in your faith journey. How has it grown or changed over the past few weeks?
9. In what ways has your study of Fire in My Bones helped you to discover the faith to be free and grow?

_____

_____

_____

A CLOSING ACTIVITY

Religious language is very important to us. It symbolizes our understanding of what is ultimately important and helps to clarify our relationships to each other. We invest our religious words with great meaning and power. The use of such language can form the basis for strong commitments and relationships. It can foster a positive self-image which, in turn, can have positive impact on others with whom we interact—both inside and outside our faith communities.

Although we cannot necessarily change the way other persons use their religious language, we can dialogue with them in the pursuit of common understanding and clarification. Specifically, we can do two things. These constitute not only a closing activity for this resource, but a continuing activity which can have far-reaching effects.

In discussing subjects with other persons where religious language is used try to do the following:

1. Listen to what words they use; but do more than this—listen to the actual *meanings* of the words they use. Look for differences between the two considerations. What feelings are being expressed by the words? What is the actual nature of the experience they are trying to convey to you?
2. Say what you really mean. Know the definitions of your words. Remember any synonyms that might help to clarify what you wish to say. In particular, use the words you have considered in this study in the way which is most appropriate. If your listener does not understand, take time to explain.

A responsible and intentional approach to the use of religious language may improve our communication, form a common base of understanding, and strengthen our faith commitments to others. This, certainly, is one hope for a study of this resource.